The Economics of Order
and Disorder

The Economics of Order and Disorder

The Market as Organizer and Creator

JACQUES LESOURNE

CLARENDON PRESS · OXFORD

1992

Oxford University Press, Walton Street, Oxford OX2 6DP
Oxford New York Toronto
Delhi Bombay Calcutta Madras Karachi
Petaling Jaya Singapore Hong Kong Tokyo
Nairobi Dar es Salaam Cape Town
Melbourne Auckland
and associated companies in
Berlin Ibadan

Oxford is a trade mark of Oxford University Press

Published in the United States
by Oxford University Press, New York

British Library Cataloguing in Publication Data
Data available

Library of Congress Cataloging-in-Publication Data
Lesourne, Jacques, 1928–
[Economie de l'ordre et du désordre. English]
The economics of order and disorder: the market as organizer and
creator / Jacques Lesourne.
p. cm.
Translation of: Economie de l'ordre et du désordre.
Includes bibliographical references and index.
1. Microeconomics. I. Title.
HB173.L6413 1990 338.5—dc20 91–34279
ISBN 0–19–828739–9

Typeset by Hope Services (Abingdon) Ltd.
Printed in Great Britain by
Biddles Ltd,
Guildford & King's Lynn

**To Pierre Massé
in remembrance**

Acknowledgements

On the threshold of this book, which stems very largely from the research carried on for a decade at the Laboratoire d'Économétrie du Conservatoire National des Arts et Métiers, I wish to thank Hélène Caron-Salmona, Gilbert Laffond, and Jean-François Laslier who collaborated with efficiency and perseverance on this attempt at elaborating a theory on self-organization in economics.

J. L.

Contents

Introduction

To the reader curious about the contents of this book, I propose a twofold answer. It is a book with a dual purpose. In the context of economic theory, it strives to bring out a paradigm capable of enlarging the set of interpretable facts, thanks to more pertinent models of interaction among the agents. It is, moreover, not a completed work but a work in the making. Its main objective is to stimulate research which might with time lead to a veritable reconstruction of micro-economic theory. This theory has, during the last half-century, progressed tremendously, thanks to the paradigm of neo-classical equilibrium. But it continues, by the very hypotheses of its models, to eliminate essential questions from the scope of reflection.

What have we, the economic theorists, to say about the economic development and decline of regions or nations? About the progressive polarization of geographic spaces? About the decline or success of enterprises? About the conditions necessary for the emergence of dominant firms? About the discovery and diffusion of innovations? About the perenniality or dynamic differentiation of markets? About the historic transformation of sociological, economic, and political modes of regulation? The lack of appropriate models makes it impossible for us to organize the vast knowledge collected in bits over two centuries on these broad subjects. Thus we can only falteringly answer the multiple questions which society puts to us: how can a nation be kept in the lead in a technology? Should it take a national policy of aid to research? Should ministries of industry be done away with? How can the decadence of a region or country be stopped? What is the use of a policy of national and regional development? How can underdevelopment be vanquished? Does opening up to the world market help a poor economy get off the ground?

All these questions have a common core. They all refer to forming behaviour, establishing relations among agents, drawing up rules, and elaborating institutions. In short, to the eventual emergence of an order, its adaptation, its transformation, its ultimate dissolution into chaos. It is hopeless, however, to try to find answers within the present conceptual framework of micro-economics.

This is the observation which engendered the writing of this book, a book whose purpose may be summed up in a single phrase: starting with the notion of self-organization, it aims to analyse the operation and the demise of institutions in economics.

To start with a banal observation which has been around for years: though everything takes place in time, the hard core of economic theory is ignorant of history. This statement, like every concise expression, deserves some explanation. The reference to history does not refer to the succession of events which took place yesterday but rather evokes the process by which time transforms a multiplicity of possible futures into a unique past. Processes in which, along with chance, and necessity as in biology, we find the expression of human will-power and the projects which man attempts to write into the future. Chance, necessity, and human will form a trilogy of creation and destruction, of change and permanence, adaptation and petrification.

What is chance? It is omnipresent in economic life: when an enterprise makes an investment, an insurer a contract, an individual a financial placement; when a worker finds a job, a buyer a product, a banker a new form of loan, a researcher a technical procedure, a director a company to take over. Invariably, whatever follows the present situation will be marked by chance.

As for necessity, it has enjoyed recognition for its role from the very beginning of the science of economics, whether it be the constraints resulting from the quantity of resources, the technical production functions of a firm, or the budget available to a household. It is necessity which connects the variables within the framework of deterministic relations.

Finally, the human will separates the human sciences from the physical sciences, replacing the passive elements with actors capable of adopting an infinitely varied selection of behaviours ranging from simple adaptation to the past to the elaboration of anticipations, to the forming of projects, to the following of strategies.

Certainly chance, necessity, and will are not totally absent from contemporary economic theory, but what has not been explored are the consequences of their interaction. This reference to theory illustrates that the remark made about the absence of history does not apply to the science of economics in its entirety, that immense

Balkanized corpus sheltering in its numerous niches knowledge of unequal solidity, but rather to the formalized part of that science, with its tightly woven relations between the axioms and the consequences, and to the very centre of the hard core of economics, the concept of equilibrium.

The archetype is the Arrow–Debreu equilibrium (Arrow and Debreu 1954, Debreu 1959), the modern version of Walrasian equilibrium (Walras 1874) and the fixed point of a model in which the givens are goods with their markets, individuals with their preferences, firms with their objectives, and production functions: the imposing of agents, the granting of institutions, goals not elaborated, paths left unexplored. An equilibrium which, in the absence of a past and a future, strangely resembles that of static mechanics.

Certainly, in the last twenty years, the perfect equilibrium of competition has given birth to a number of descendants: fixed price equilibria with rationing, temporary equilibria, permanent or growth path equilibria, signalling equilibria, and multiple equilibria of the game theory and of imperfect competition. But, in most cases, the equilibrium is not the culminating point of a history; it simply characterizes situations in which no actor wishes to modify his behaviour given his environment and information.

As soon as it departs from the privileged field of equilibria, economic theory is ill at ease. Has it not often burdened itself with its own Maxwell demon, the officiating Walras auctioneer who proposes prices, registers the offers and demands, and lets the markets open only when, for all goods, the quantities demanded are equal to the quantities offered?

That is why I spoke of the ignorance of history. It is of course not total, and there are brilliant exceptions which I shall come back to in a moment, but these scattered islets never manage to enlarge and agglomerate into the beginnings of a continent. In the great symphony concert of equilibrium, the discordant voices of self-organization, of the dialectic of order and disorder can hardly be heard. Discordant? The word lends confusion, for it is far from my mind to imitate the iconoclasts. I value the benefits of the paradigm of equilibrium too much to uproot it. All the more so as it is possible to integrate it into the larger paradigm to which this book is devoted.

Before attempting to do this, however, two more preliminary remarks are in order. First of all, my aim is not to introduce into the discipline of economics any foreign notions, artifical grafts condemned to wither on the vine, for they ignore the existing problematics and do not fit into the conceptual framework already constructed. Nor, in the second place, is it my aim to add yet another layer to the immense amount of 'soft' literature—in the Anglo-Saxon sense of soft science—which already floods economics on the subject. It is, after all, highly useful literature, since it contributed to highlighting most of the phenomena which should be analysed. What I propose, on the contrary, is to develop, in an endogenous manner, reflection on self-organization in economics. Starting with the theory of micro-economics itself, I hope to build precise models based on explicit hypotheses, and thus draw out the significance of the propositions obtained.

This situates my work at the confluence of several streams of scientific thought.

1. The first belongs to the general theory of systems. It is the one which, from von Bertalanffy (1968) to Ashby (1952, 1956), from Mesarovic (1961) to Beer (1959, 1966), from Bateson (1951) to Simon (1957), from Easton (1965) to Deutsch (1963), from Prigogine (1962) to von Foerster (1960), from Atlan (1972) to Morin (1977), from Varela (1979) to Maturana (1970)—to mention only a few names—has been concerned with the properties of those strange beings, sets of elements linked by sets of relations. It has shown how, marvellously but without mystery, one could, by degrees, rise from simple systems with few properties, just good enough to transform inputs into outputs, to cybernetic systems supposedly self-regulating thanks to feedbacks; then, from learning systems able to modify their relations by taking advantage of experience, to self-organizing systems capable of setting goals, inventing, and creating, to wind up in the end with 'societies' of systems, that uniting of complex systems communicating among themselves (Lesourne 1976).

It was systematic problematics which made it possible to understand the relations of order and disorder. Of course, since Carnot and Boltzmann, it has been known that the entropy of a closed system can but increase and that any isolated organization consequently has a tendency to self-destruct and return to chaos. But what examples drawn from physics, chemistry, and biology have shown is that, locally, disorder could give rise to an open organization, capable, thanks to feedbacks, of using chance to maintain and develop itself. In other words, under certain conditions, a self-organizing system is capable of constituting itself out of chaos and perpetuating itself in that environment by re-establishing if necessary its organization and even improving it through random attempts.

Thus this approach invites scientists to shift the object of their investigations from the operation of institutions to the creation of the same. From that point on, equilibrium only holds meaning in relation to the history which brings it into being or to the future which threatens it with destruction. A change in structure which profoundly modifies all of micro-economics.[1]

2. As for the second stream, it has long meandered through the Amazon of the science of economics. Has it not been said that it was in reading Malthus that Darwin got the idea of natural selection?[2] Hardly surprising, moreover, seeing that from the *Wealth of Nations* by Adam Smith to the *Principles of Economy* by Alfred Marshall, an implicit theory of evolution constantly shows up in the writings of economists. Even Karl Marx, when he deduced his dynamics of the Hegelian dialectic of contradiction and conflicts, integrated the process of evolution into his analysis. It was the work of Walras which was to consecrate the separation of the mainstream of dominant economic theory from the wash of evolutionist models. And no doubt the split was a happy once since it made it possible for economics to build the Newtonian statics and dynamics which it could hardly do without.

But the evolutionist current has never disappeared. It is present in the work of Schumpeter who, from *The Theory of Economic Development* (1912) to *Capitalism, Socialism and Democracy* (1942) never ceases to emphasize the mutational consequences of inventions and innovations, the central role of entrepreneurs, and the emergence and decline of economic institutions. It is present in works of authors as diverse as Knight (1921), von Hayek (1945), Alchian (1950), Rosenberg (1976), Freeman (1974), Perroux (1975), Eliasson (1977), Futia (1980), and Witt (1986*a*, 1986*b*). Special mention should be made of the Nelson and Winters book, *An Evolutionary Theory of Economic Change* (1982).

Evolutionist problematics rightly emphasize the constant inter-

---

[1] For simplicity's sake I have included in the systemic current the very interesting work of J. P. Dupuy and his team at CREA. For the bibliography I have selected out of this abundant work two texts from 1982 and 1988.

[2] On the relationship between economics and the theory of evolution, see particularly Boulding (1981).

action between the agents' search for new opportunities and the engendering of such opportunities through innovation. As seen from this approach an economy is constantly in the making: a random development since it depends on individual or company discoveries. This being so, the very notion of economic equilibrium is meaningless and Nelson and Winters are right to emphasize the breach which separates their conceptual framework from orthodox theory.

This book very largely adopts an evolutionist view, but it does not, as we shall see, rule out a place for the notion of equilibrium— or, even better, stability.

3. A third current to which this work owes a good deal is the behaviourist approach. Following the lead of Herbert Simon in *Models of Man* (1957), this approach focuses on the limited rationality of behaviour. Faced with real problems too difficult for them, firms do not attempt to maximize their profits on a combination of all the possibilities, but content themselves with satisfactory rules of decision-making, which generally allow them to progress and survive (Cyert and March 1963). With the first few chapters of this book, we shall see how inevitable the behaviourist approach is, given the complexity of economic systems in evolution, but we shall also take stock of difficulties which it brings up in authorizing a wide range of behaviours.

4. Institutional economics constitutes another current from which we draw inspiration. Following Commons (1934) and Coase (1937), Williamson (1975) contributed to its development. The central idea is the following:

(1) Markets and firms are interchangeable instruments for the execution of a set of transactions; (2) carrying out a set of transactions through markets or within a firm depends upon the relative efficiency of each mode; (3) the cost of drawing up and carrying out complex contracts by way of the markets depends for one thing on the characteristics of the decision-makers involved in the transaction and for another thing on the properties of the market; (4) although the human and environmental factors hampering exchanges between firms (on the market) show up somewhat differently within a firm, they are the same in both cases. A symmetric analysis of commercial relations therefore assumes acceptance of both the origins of the market deficiencies and the transitional limits of internal organizations. (Williamson 1975: 8)

By focusing on the parallels between hierarchies and markets, Williamson deserves credit for emphasizing the central role of institutions in resolving the economic problems of allocation, production, and distribution. Although his analysis belongs essentially to comparative statics, it leads to important questions of self-organization. How can a market disappear giving birth to a unique organization? How can an economic hierarchy collapse in engendering a market? In such evolutions the forces at work will, moreover, largely be those identified by Williamson.

5. Finally, the last current springs from economic theory itself, but it appears in fragments as if there were no links between the components. Hence, only as the arguments in the book develop, will a framework stand out uniting some of the most interesting theoretical research of the last thirty years. The stimulating work of Jacob Marschak and Roy Radner (1972) on the functioning of teams, the research by Stigler (1961) on information economics, the analyses by Stiglitz (1979), Salop and Stiglitz (1982), Diamond (1971), and Fisher (1970, 1973) on market equilibrium and imperfect information, the introduction by Akerlof (1970), Radner (1979), and a few others of the problematics of rational expectations in micro-economics, the development of the signalling theory by Spence (1974), the literature on the process of bilateral negotiation (Lainé 1987) and the introduction of the B-process by Hurwicz, Radner, and Reiter (1975), the surplus theory by Allais (1981), the explosion of research on repeated games, and the appearance of the contract theory. It is not an exhaustive list but it is most impressive, and shows that, even if the paradigm of self-organization is not yet recognized in economic theory, signs of its coming are surfacing in many places. Indeed, in nearly all these works, economic agents strive to acquire information, and then, by their behaviour in making use of that information, create a specific equilibrium. They therefore turn information into organization.

These instances in no way constitute a 'survey'. They aim, at most, at identifying the main roots of our thought and at situating our procedure within the framework of economic science. But what is meant by self-organization? Rigour is not the rule at this point. So for the moment it is enough that this term serve to designate the possibility for a system to acquire new properties by itself organizing or modifying its organization. The enterprise which succeeds in structuring competition, the market which gives rise to new markets, the employment system which creates unions, the urban or national economy which becomes the centre of a world economy, are all showing proof of such a capacity.

What are the minimal requirements for a system to present self-organizing properties? The best way to answer this question is to cite Prigogine and Stengers (1988). Even though they had physical systems in mind, their reflection remains perfectly valid for economic systems. They show that there are three minimal requirements:

The first of these requirements, nearly tautological, is certainly irreversibility, that is to say *the break in symmetry between the before and after*.

A second requirement is then that we may give meaning to the notion of an *event*. An event can only by definition be deduced from a determinist law: it implies in one way or another that what happened 'might' not have happened, it therefore brings us back to possibilities which no form of knowledge could reduce. The intelligibility mode of the possibles as such and the events which decide among the possibles is by definition the probabilistic description. However, the probabilistic laws in themselves are not yet sufficient. Any history, any narrative implies these events, implies that something happened which might not have happened, but it holds no interest unless these events *carry meaning*. A series of dice throws is not worth mentioning unless certain throws have significant consequences: dice are an instrument of games of chance only when there are *stakes in the game*.

The third minimal requirement is therefore that certain events may supposedly *change the meaning* of the evolution that they stress, as it can be said in turn that the evolution should be characterized by mechanisms or relationships which may supposedly impart meaning to the event, to create *new coherences* from it.

These three requirements will seem very clear in certain models in this book, but when found in economic systems they are perceived through a certain number of elements which nearly always condition the alchemical mechanisms of self-organization: friction (or in other words irreversibility), uncertainty, complexity, the more or less limited rationality of the actors, their opportunism, their number, the exchange of information among them.

Friction! I can still hear my theoretical mechanics professor explaining that without the forces it engenders cars and trains would spin their wheels and buildings collapse. Lacking in elementary mechanics, friction is just as absent from the Walrasian equilibrium which presupposes flexible prices, interchangeable consumption, or production factors. Even so its role is every bit as important in economics as in physics since it guarantees in the same manner the sustaining of situations which, in the world of perfect reversibility, would dissolve into thin air. But its existence must first be recognized in its multiple forms.

One form of friction is the investment made in view of future savings or benefits and which introduces discontinuity between the ex-ante and ex-post situations. In the ex-ante situation, its size might prevent the future creation of a production capacity, the training of employees, a change of address for a family, the closing of a firm, or lay-offs of its personnel.[3] In the ex-post situation, investing may make it possible to dispose of new resources.

Another form of friction is the constraint which renders impossible or costly the discovery of information, the diffusion of knowledge, access to a rare resource, or the use of production combinations. While yet another form of friction is the conservative psychological attitude which devalues initiative, privileges that which exists, depreciates the future, and reinforces memory of past experiences.

Thanks to friction innovation is preserved, organization kept up, and permanence maintained. It must never be forgotten that economic dynamics are dynamics of irreversible phenomena and that it is this irreversibility which lends stability to the structures on which development is founded.

But there would be no creation without uncertainty: without the chance influences emanating from the actors or the environment. Actors gnawed by curiosity, who invent solutions, who experiment with rules of conduct, who forget, who adapt their preferences, who meet, associate, and separate. Actors whose random interaction shakes up existing organizations and gives birth to new ones. An environment which upsets prices, makes quantities uncertain, mixes noise in with information, stirs up new challenges, and destroys the actors themselves.

We shall run into this surprising couple, chance and friction, on nearly every page. A source of threat because of the problems it brings up and the burdens it imposes, this relationship is at the same time a source of autonomy thanks to the leeway it creates and the protections it offers. Let friction win out and the system at risk of collapsing will maintain its organization in spite of everything. Let

---

[3] The costs of closings and lay-offs can indeed be considered an investment since they make it possible to reduce future losses.

chance triumph and it will multiply haphazard experiences or fluctuate with incoming winds.

To the economist, as to the physical chemist, introducing chance at the agent level poses the tricky problem of a double modelization of reality. Indeed, he needs to reason, on the one hand, on a microscopic representation which is in a way analogous to Boltzmannian statistics,[4] and, on the other, build macroscopic dynamics which constitute the counterpart to classic thermodynamics. Going from one to the other is not the easiest task there is.

Complexity is an ingredient which appears in even the simplest model of market dynamics. This complexity is masked in models of general equilibrium for they are only interested in cases where the prices already formed sum up for each individual the information on the whole system. But this nice transparence crumbles from the moment that there exist as many prices as contracts and that each actor is confronted with only a few offers which change from period to period. It is impossible thereafter to describe the system simply. Its complexity becomes such that each agent has only imperfect and partial knowledge. Nevertheless, out of all this chaos there may arise an order (a set of prices, for example) under the effect of a multitude of independent actions.

Complexity and uncertainty imply the following element, the more or less limited rationality of the actors. An element which throws off-course a neo-classical economist used to maximizing utilities in simple informational contexts and which is indispensable for three reasons.

1. What would a theory be worth if it based the operation and the make-up of economic institutions solely on actors endowed with the possibility of carrying out infinite calculations and of having complete preferences? Besides, such a postulate would be all the more pernicious since it would mask a fundamental property of self-organization processes: their being more or less robust according to the agents' ability to process information. Thus, while certain dynamics of imperfect competition are only conceivable with firms able to determine all the strategies of response to others, it hardly takes a superman, in general, to make a market work. Is it not

---

[4] Reference to an analogy should not put out of mind the major differences which separate economic agents from molecules and the existence in economics of 'non atomic' agents, that is to say those whose size is out of all proportion compared to the others.

enough in many cases that individuals be content with reacting afterwards to a situation which they observe? Nothing is also more useful than to be able to recognize the processes which might turn out differently simply because of the presence of agents more active or astute than the others.

In this respect, the debate in economics which opposes advocates of satisfaction thresholds and those upholding maximization of utility under constraint seems to me to result from an error in perspective. The essential point lies not in choosing the right model since from one individual to another the refinement of behaviour may run from one extreme to the other. It lies in exploring the sensitivity of self-organization phenomena with regard to the strategies the agents adopt.

2. At any rate, the presence of a number of individuals with limited rationality exerts a profound influence on the evolution of economic systems. Faced with the complexity of their environment, these individuals largely unarmed, are content with contributing to short-term regulation by acting on the variables which might tend to depart from the desired range or which set off far-reaching trans-formations whose direction and extent escape them. It is then possible that behaviour which is natural in a limited horizon and within the framework of simplified representations leads in the long term to abrupt discontinuities. How could we fail to mention here the unexpected adverse effects most often brought on by economic or political decisions (Boudon 1977).

3. Finally, were we to regret all limited rationality, it would frequently be quite difficult to build models on the behaviour of the perfect actor of the neo-classical theory. In the course of dynamic evolution, does their environment not modify itself unendingly while their information is limited to scattered fragments? Hence the impossibility—at this stage of research—of escaping from *ad hoc* hypotheses to describe agents' choices. But nothing hinders the retaining of plausible hypotheses until the day when it will be possible to replace them with more extensive behaviour axioms which will be not only sufficient but necessary.

The limited rationality of the actors does not exclude what Williamson calls opportunism, that is, the propensity of certain individuals to falsify information or to refuse to execute a contract whenever they find it in their interest. That possibility, which the science of economics formerly ignored, is now explicitly taken into account: either in the repetitive game theory where co-operation does not stem from any particular initial agreement but from the interests of each player at the time, or in the contract theory in which revealing the truth is the best solution for the player who possesses all the information. In all evidence, actors' opportunism plays a role in self-organizational phenomena as it influences the recourse to the market or the hierarchy in order to carry out certain transactions.

That the number of agents be introduced at this point is no surprise to an economist. Has micro-economic theory from the very beginning not distinguished between models in which each individual finds himself faced with an environment and those in which his will opposes the plans of competitors or adversaries? That distinction retains its full value in self-organization since, depending on the system considered, his future may or may not depend on the competence of the individuals which he brings into play. Thus the random end result of processes of oligopolistic competition is often influenced by the capabilities of the group of leaders selected within the firms. In other words, the approach adopted in this book helps us to understand why the appearance of exceptional figures may modify the course of history or not have the least effect on it.

There remains the last element on our list: exchanges of information. Its presence here should not be surprising. Have we not known since the time of Leon Brillouin (1949) that the use of information may give birth to organization and that any organization in return may send messages to its environment? An observation of which economics offers us numerous examples: how could a firm build up its clientele without making its products known, a person find a job without information on positions available, a board of directors function without exchanges of information? But as long as economists did not get beyond these obvious facts, the role played by information in the economic paradigm remained marginal. The breakthrough only came the day a precise description was made of the imperfect and incomplete knowledge to which each agent had access, in which the means of acquiring new information was defined, in which a place was made for the voluntary manipulation of signals by the senders. As a consequence it can be seen throughout the book that the fine structures of information in economics often determine the outcome of self-organization processes.

In this way we will show that the economics of order and disorder, of creation and ossification, are woven from chance, complexity, more or less doubtful exchanges of information, more or less rational and opportunist behaviour, and greater or lesser social and economic inflexibility.

Let us now make room for the programme. It is very useful to have one in order to situate progress in research at all times, even if its size does go beyond reason, and if thought, like love, knows no laws. One remark is in order before presenting it, a remark which has no other purpose but to emphasize that any analysis is based, as is customary in micro-economics, on the postulate of methodological individualism dear to Raymond Boudon.[5] In all the models, it will be individuals who act. By participating in firms. By associating to form unions. By applying for jobs. By operating on behalf of the State. Whether they do so by imitating, being influenced, or internalizing solidarities, will in no way change their nature as ultimate components, like the atom in traditional chemistry.

The programme, as it appears to me today, should link six successive parts. The present volume combines the first two which form a whole since they deal with the market. The second volume could theoretically be devoted to centralized organization (the third part), while the last volume would deal with the fourth, fifth, and sixth parts.

1. Priority will first be given to the market, that institution which classifies and organizes and whose origin seems to go back to the very beginnings of history. First of all, just how does it work, this market, the mysteries of which our grandfathers were thought to have elucidated, when we think only of small-sized sellers and buyers seeking each other? Be it the labour-market or the consumer goods market, which processes of search, negotiation, and adaptation of demands assure its convergence towards a single price, and which single price would that be? Faced with random shocks from outside, is it capable, like a cell, of restoring its membrane, of reconstituting the sorting of offers and demands adopted or rejected?

To what degree is it perturbed by irreversibilities of all sorts: recruitment or lay-off expenses, constraints on information, the cost of research, the inflexibility of expectations, lethargic behaviour, the existence of increasing yields? How might its evolution be affected by the existence of signals, transmitted purposely or not by

[5] 'Individualism et holism dans les sciences sociales', in Birnbaum and Lecas 1986.

agents, imperfectly revealing the quality of the goods or services offered? How does it behave when the seller can adapt at every period not only the price proposed but the quantity put on the market as well?

Six chapters will make up this first part. The first will present the building of the hypotheses which make it possible to outline this set of models. The second will describe a very simple market without friction in which buyers and sellers are only interested in one unit of goods. The third will introduce in the form of costs the existence of irreversibles. The fourth will allow increasing yields for sellers. The fifth will introduce sellers able to act both on the price and the quantity at the same time. Finally, the sixth will touch on the revelation through prices of information on the quality of the goods exchanged.

Through this analysis of the market by its functions of classification and organization, we shall be confronted for the first time with the economic mechanisms of the emergence of order from disorder. It will therefore be essential to delve deeper into their significance and to evaluate the limits of the results obtained.

2. If the random dynamics of the market were to engender only prices and the sorting of offers and demands, its properties of self-organization would appear particularly poor. But such is not the case. In the course of its history and during the functioning of the same, a market may give rise to the creation of intermediaries, the elaboration of opinions and theories, the founding of unions, the concentration of the productive apparatus, the birth of new products, the forming of more qualified workers, and the emergence of new markets. In other words, interaction between the agents within the framework of the market is liable to generate, in an endogenous manner, a whole range of institutions. Here we are then in the presence of processes of self-organization of a higher order than the simple convergence of a market towards an organized stable state. It will be necessary, therefore, to study the corresponding phenomena in some depth.

This second part, devoted to the creative market, will include five chapters which will deal successively with the birth of intermediaries, the forming of opinions, the generating of skills, the founding of unions, and the evolution of the structures of competition.

3. Attention should then be focused on centralized organization (hierarchy), that rival of the market whose first appearance stretches

back into the mists of time. Faced with uncertainties from without and resistance by members from within, how can it ensure its permanence? How can it adapt in step with its development? How does it go about elaborating the rules for decision-making which allow the management of its essential resources: the amount of human resources, the stock of raw materials, the quantity of cash, the extent of knowledge, the size of the clientele? Which challenges might it respond to with brutal mutations or minor adaptations? Which are the shake-ups that would condemn it to death? Does internal friction reduce its chances of survival?

We shall thus quite naturally be led to wonder about the existence (postulated by Edgar Morin in 1977) of an anti-organization within the body of all organizations and on the role that this anti-organization is liable to play in crisis situations.

4. At this stage in the thought process, all the elements should be united to enable us to pursue the relations between the market and the hierarchy. These are complex relations since either one may develop at the expense of the other or arise from the disintegration of the other, but they may also coexist in symbiosis. In that case, there are actors operating on the market who, like firms, in themselves constitute central organizations and who, by their size, have a wide range of strategies available to them. Hence it is a problematic related to that proposed by Alexis Jacquemin in *Sélection et pouvoir dans la nouvelle économie industrielle* (1986).

To what extent does history modify the outcome of competition among firms differing in effectiveness? What influence do company strategies exert on the evolution of the structures of competition? How does interference between these structures and internal company organization modify the productive apparatus of a national economy? All are crucial questions since dynamic interaction between firms, serving as the warp of the fabric of innovation and creation, allows any human group more or less to transform its virtual potentialities into realities.

5. What about the penultimate step? It could be devoted to the use of geographic space. That self-organization is at work is impossible to deny, so blinding is the evidence. Even the most convinced apostle of the uniqueness of equilibrium is forced to recognize in the growth and decline of cities the mark of history, that is, for those who prefer the geographer's vocabulary, the consequence of structural decisions. That is why the study of the localization of human

activities seems, for traditional micro-economics, to be a strange chapter indeed, with its irreversibilities, its economies of scale, its externalities, and its non-convexities. There is nothing of the like in the present programme, for the paradigm which inspired it naturally introduces the problematics of territorial development.

The central question is contained in two sentences: to what forms of space utilization (the plural is imperative) might individual, company, and public group strategies lead? What would be the consequences thereof in terms of externalities, positive or negative?

6. There remains one last group of questions. No one will be surprised to learn that they concern the relations between the firm, the market, and the State. Here we are at the heart of problems fundamental to all modern societies—in the West as in the East.

How, in Western societies, does an individual vote incite a government to make its weight felt on market dynamics, to modify revenue distribution, to define the offer of public goods, and to remove productive activities from competition? How, in planned economies (or those in the course of deplanification), are goals set forth, regulation mechanisms set up, adverse effects of centralization fought off, and resistance to change eliminated?

Needless to say we can—at best—only study a few of these problems, but the analysis should make it possible to illustrate the importance of self-organization in the interaction between micro-economics and political power.

This programme is obviously too vast. Nevertheless, the idea is not to carry it out completely—such an ambition would be puerile—but to show by outlining it that an approach in terms of self-organization, bringing into play chance, necessity, and human will all at once, allows us to resituate micro-economics in a conceptual framework which is both richer and more satisfying. It is up to the reader to judge, upon finishing this volume, whether this new paradigm seems useful to him for future ventures into the science of economics.

Part I
The Market as Organizer

1

Building the Models

This first chapter will help me place the two parts of this book. It is itself divided into two sections.

● The first concerns individuals. How can those individuals who leave their specific imprint on economic and social self-organization, those individuals who are motors for change and brakes on adaptation, be fitted into a model? How can their choices and their behaviour be represented? That is the question for which I should like to try to draft a rough answer, adequate for the reflections in the present work.

● The second section enumerates the hypotheses structuring the field of research explored in the chapters which follow which must subsequently be called on to define the characteristics of the main families of models.

Individual Behaviour

It is useful first to distinguish, as Walliser (1985) does, between three possible environments for the individual: the passive, which is independent of individual behaviour, the reactive, which responds in a mechanical way to this behaviour, and, finally, the active environment, which in addition follows its own decision-making process. Both parts of this book ignore game situations. It is therefore sufficient to deal with the dimensions of individual behaviour in a passive or reactive environment.

One fact is evident, since self-organization is a dynamic process, that it is first of all within a temporal perspective that individual choices must be described. Choices, which are made at a particular moment, but in relation to knowledge of the present, experience of the past, and representation of the futures. Choices which it is convenient to separate—in the purest tradition of economic science—into operational choices and choices of investment, the first having only short-term effects on the individual's situation, the second determining his future.

The distinction between operation and investment naturally depends on the model in question. Thus in a model on the labour-market in which an individual goes job-hunting then applies for one of the positions he has found, the decision to look for a job is an investment decision, that of applying is an operational decision.

With the development of economics there has been no end to the enrichment of the nature of choices possible whether they be of the investment or operation type. To the earlier decisions on consumption have been added choices on roles and decisions made within the context of those roles, whether they concern the search for information, the distribution of resources, the drawing up of rules (such as contracts), the determining of the amount of effort to be made, or the revealing of intentionally true or false data.

Operational choices

For operational choices, nothing is more natural than to use the core of decision theory: a set of possible choices, a representation of the environment, conjectures as to the consequences of those choices in that environment, an order of preference on the consequences, a process of decision selection.

To speak of a set of possible choices is also to speak of the constraints which limit these choices. These constraints depend not only on today's environment but also on yesterday's investment choices. Should the pertinent decision not have been made earlier, then today's individual is unable to react. Should an effort of imagination, research, or training have been granted formerly, then an individual disposes of a wide range of strategies.

With the representation of the environment comes the cleavage between reality of that environment—or at least the description given by a model builder—and the way the individual perceives it. Indeed, the hypothesis of rational expectations which postulates the identity of these two models evidently corresponds only to a marginal case which is hardly in line with the inspiration of this book.

The model retained by the actor will be rooted in available information; hence the double problem of the nature and origin of this information: is it a question of common knowledge which a group of actors share and know to share? Is it a question of imperfect or incomplete data specific to an actor? Is it a question of elements recently obtained by direct transmission or progressively elaborated through learning?

The hypothesis of limited rationality will generally lend a simple form to the modelling of the environment: thus an individual who during his last T observations has not found a position available offering remuneration higher than x, will postulate that he will not get more than x during the next period; a manufacturer who has observed price p_t for period t will assume that this price is still valid for the period $(t + 1)$.

It is within the framework of this modelling, generally very simple, that conjectures on the consequences of individual choices are formed through a process in which reasoning rests upon learning since the individual starts by committing to memory the succession of his choices, their effects, and the conjectures that he had made, before postulating the consequences of his decisions of exploitation.[1] In so doing, the individual sets up an experience memory, the depth of which may be defined as the number of past periods considered in elaborating the conjectures. From then on, the shorter the memory horizon, the less the individual will be able to learn. The stronger the connection between past observations and present conjectures, the less attention the individual will pay to recent information indicating ruptures in the evolution of the environment.

At this stage also, limited rationality leaves its mark: thus in one of the models developed we shall accept that a manager who at a certain level of production observed a drop in profits when he increased his price will not repeat the experience at the same price and same level of production.

Several remarks must be made concerning preferences. It is first of all important to emphasize the fact that they are firmly rooted in individual history, a history marked by the influence of its former states. One might speak of a preference memory and introduce the depth of the memory, that is the number of periods whose past state conditions present preferences. The past does not model only the contents of the preferences. If one admits the notion of cardinal utility it also modifes the level of present satisfaction through the

---

[1] He may also take into account information on the success and failures of other actors.

comparison which the individual makes with past satisfactions. The consequences in terms of self-organization are obvious:

- being accustomed to a certain behaviour slows down the shift in choices when the environment changes, gives other agents the time to adapt, and reinforces the chances of survival of present structures or institutions;
- on the other hand, the accumulation of discontent may suddenly be expressed as an irreversible and brutal rejection which contributes to shaking up the existing order in an unexpected manner.

But emphasis must also be placed on the desire to imitate or the frustration a person may feel upon observing the situation of others within or without his own social groups. Hence the phenomena of behaviour diffusion within a population, phenomena which, according to the hypotheses made, may abort or spread like wildfire.

And finally, in an uncertain environment, individual preferences bring into play not only a wage level, an amount of profits, and quantities consumed, but the life expectancy of the organizations in which the individual participates. Of course, profits and survival are not always antinomic and, when they are, the economic agents accept arbitrating between them. There is no doubt, nevertheless, that economics very largely underestimates the importance of survival behaviour where companies are concerned.

Still to be defined is the process of choice-making. With the exception of a few heterodox thinkers, economics has always represented this process as a maximization under constraints thus giving the individual an infinite number of computational possibilities. Nevertheless, does present observation not show, day after day, that individuals prefer empirical rules leading to progressive, local improvement of their utility? To the point that the high-sounding name of 'artificial intelligence' now designates the computer programmes which simulate such rules of decision-making.

What do we know of these processes? Numerous works by psychologists or sociologists have shown that most often agents:

- do not immediately adapt to changes observed or anticipated in the environment;
- proceed by improving on the situation they have to start with and therefore carry on an oriented search;

- make only partial use of the possibilities the environment offers them, being content with satisfactory solutions;
- frequently use random attempts to explore the set of possibles.

In some cases, the choice-making processes permit the individual to solve empirically the maximization problems traditional in micro-economics and to reach the situations of equilibrium expected, but in other cases they are caught in sub-optimal traps or brought to ruin. The rest of the book will allow us to illustrate these diverse possibilities.

Investment choices

Let us now consider investment choices. In the first place, in the economics of order and disorder, investment may take on extra-ordinarily different forms: a search for information on the prices proposed, stochastic transformation of individual skills through training, modification through the publicity of the perception or the expectations of other actors, research and development expenditures which bring about random discovery of innovations. What is more, the effects of investment are nearly always uncertain since they happen in the future. Thus it seems that investment is one of the principal sources of the creation of order and disorder in the economic system.

A second observation is quite banal. Investment choices first show up in the form of a cost—monetary or psychological—which has to be deducted from the satisfactions of the moment: the cost of information or of the search for solutions, the cost of professional training or mobility, of acquiring lodgings, or a change of location. The end result is that investment behaviour continuously exhibits discontinuities. If the decision comes down to two possibilites 'to invest' or 'not to invest' an individual will abruptly stop investing as soon as the expected increase in utility drops below the cost level. There is another consequence: members of the same group, con-fronted with analogous choices, will reveal qualitatively different behaviour—some will invest, others not. For example, on the labour-market, where individuals must accept some cost in order to draw a selection of positions, the dynamics of the market will progressively separate the participants into two groups: active ones who will continue job-hunting indefinitely and passive ones who, after an undetermined period of time, will content themselves with the salary they are getting. Of course, such facts are acknowledged by economics, but in a way they play a marginal role, even though it is indispensable to take them into account in order to understand how economic institutions come into being.

A third observation is just as banal: an individual, however limited his rationality may be, will not be able to escape comparisons of immediate cost and possible future advantages of investment. Hence he needs to build a representation of the future—a representation both more ambitious and more simplified in relation to reality than for operational decisions. It will be more ambitious because it will have to deal simultaneously with constraints, preferences, and the environment. It will be more simplified in relation to reality because, to be usable, it will have to deduce from a few hypotheses the setting up of expectations and truncate the future, limiting itself to evaluating after a few periods the cards in hand for the more distant future. Hence the appearance of an expectation horizon defined by the number of periods that the individual explicitly takes into account.

As for ways of evaluating the consequences of investment alternatives, they will be comprised of two parts:

- judging the effects investment may have on opening the field of operational decisions in the future (a two-faced idol, investment liberates the future from past constraints even as it hems that future in with new constraints);
- estimating the direct influence of investment on the future state of the individual and on his levels of satisfaction, which supposes generally implicit hypotheses on the operational decisions.

But any investment decision implies accepting or refusing the logic of the existing system. The individual who looks for employment, who changes his residence, who tries to improve his professional skills, remains within the framework of a competitive labour-market. The one who is active in a union, fights for the regulation of lay-offs, tries to obtain a minimum wage from political powers, is, on the other hand, seeking an endogenous transformation of market organization.

At the end of this process, the last step will consist of balancing out present costs and the future levels of satisfaction which investment choices will hopefully engender. It will be done by introducing a future discount rate, that old tool from the economist's arsenal. At that point, there will appear the threshold phenomena already mentioned which, in the neighbourhood of critical values, cause the individual to shift from passiveness to searching, from acceptance to revolt.

Under these circumstances, the dynamics of an economic system are liable to engender diverse relations between stable states and hypotheses of individual behaviour. In some cases, for a wide range of behaviour, the system will converge towards a stable state, thus demonstrating exceptional resilience. In others, the nature of the stable states will be in close relation to the hypotheses retained. In the extreme, individuals forming rational expectations and endowed with infinite computational capacity will lead the system to the robust equilibria of traditional theory, while weaker hypotheses will be associated with a whole array of metastable equilibria, equilibria which, like oversaturated solutions in physics, may maintain themselves indefinitely or be abruptly destroyed by the arrival of a germ in the form of a better performing actor. However—and here economics distinguishes itself from physical chemistry—the robust equilibria are themselves not safe from innovations which may destroy them.

The reader will easily find, in each of the models developed hereafter, recourse to the concepts which have just been presented when the environment is passive or reactive. The case of an active environment requires further thought as shown by certain recent developments in game theory.

The task which now awaits us is the enumeration of the hypotheses which make it possible to define the families of dynamic market models.

Enumeration of the Hypotheses

In most of the models considered in the two parts of this book the workings of a market stem from common mechanisms: the buyers and sellers show up, make contact, gather information, anticipate, elaborate plans, negotiate, carry out transactions, and in so doing continually modify one another's information, expectations, and strategy, creating therewith dynamics which may lead, for example, either to stable states (the prices and quantities exchanged being reproduced from one period to the other), to more or less periodic fluctuations, or to endless fluctuations. Such an analysis, calling on random and dynamic processes, also makes it possible to ponder the creating of new markets from an initial market (for example, after the development of new economic agents, the progressive transformation of the goods exchanged, or the geographic relocation of buyers or sellers). In the same way, while in operation, the market may receive shocks from without or experience endogenous changes (coming from new agents or the change in demands on behalf of the buyers or sellers), such that its perenniality is threatened, without the course of history being determined. Robust for some values of the parameters, the existence of the market for other values might prove extremely fragile.

Here then is the setting: at one moment in time buyers and sellers are brought together, who, in the course of their transactions, will begin to exchange, for monetary payment, diverse quantities of one or more goods or services. Time will supposedly be divided into periods beginning from that first moment. The hypotheses to be examined for building such models successively involve the goods and services exchanged, the agents, and the market operations.

The goods and services exchanged

1. The first question is whether the actors have perfect knowledge of the characteristics of the goods exchanged. If their information is perfect their only worry will be carrying out the transaction at the best price, but, if this is not the case, they will be in a more difficult situation as they will be forced either to buy information on their characteristics or estimate them from what they know, or from what the market reveals to them.

Examples of a market with imperfect knowledge about goods and services have become commonplace: the neophyte who wants to buy a fine bottle of Bordeaux wine will agree to pay more because he supposes that under the influence of informed consumer demand the quality will increase with the price; the firm that wants to recruit an engineer will look at his diplomas (which supposedly reveal minimal competence) and his preceding salary (which no doubt expresses his employer's opinion of his abilities); the head of a factory on the point of hiring a worker often decides to have him pass a test before making a final decision.[2]

2. Supposing that the characteristics of the goods and services are perfectly well known to the actors, the second question is whether the characteristics will remain identical throughout the evolution of the market. Traditional theory has always been concerned with the first eventuality, but the second is no less realistic: an individual's professional skills change in relation to the positions he holds; firms attempt to modify their products in relation to the response from consumers; a used car depreciates all the faster when it has logged a lot of mileage. And, contrary to common usage, it does not suffice to say that there is a shift from one market to another when the product changes, because the firm might recruit either a highly skilled individual or one not so highly skilled and a buyer might be interested in either a new or a used car. In all cases, it is the initial market which, in the course of its operations, engenders successive markets.

3. Let us say that the characteristics of the goods and services exchanged remain constant. The third question then is quite familiar to economists since it deals with the conditions in which transactions are carried out, that is, with the contracts between agents. It leads to distinguishing among contracts which are to be carried out immediately (10 francs for a kilo of oranges), contracts of determined length (the hiring of a worker for six months), contracts of undetermined length (the granting of an overdraft at the bank, the hiring of a worker for an undetermined length of time), contracts for future execution (delivery of a ton of copper in three months), insurance contracts (payment of an indemnity in case of an accident), etc.—this list is obviously not exhaustive. The literature on contracts has made enormous progress in the last two decades, but problems concerning the market mechanism are complex enough to justify giving priority in this book to the simplest models, which assume that the contracts between agents are for immediate execution.

4. That leaves one last question as far as goods and services are concerned; it hardly deserves lengthy development since it only concerns the nature of the goods and services offered by the

---

[2] For models in which buyers have imperfect knowledge of the goods and services exchanged, see notably Akerlof (1970), Hey and McKenna (1981), Smallwood and Conlisk (1979). This approach leads in particular to introducing 'signal' and 'hazard moral' problems. See Riley (1979), Rothschild and Stiglitz (1976), Spence (1974).

different sellers. Goods may be imperfect substitutes or perfectly identical, though examples of imperfect substitution are numerous: cars of different makes, work services supplied by individuals of equal competence but originating within the firm or without. In what follows, we shall choose the hypothesis in which the goods and services offered by the various sellers are identical.

The agents

1. The simplest markets bring together only two categories of agents, the buyers and sellers of elementary economic theory, but reality offers a much richer range of situations: agents may specialize in gathering or diffusing information (selection agencies, market analysis firms, advertising agencies), or in purchasing or selling for others (brokers). Buyers (or sellers) may group together in coalitions which will negotiate, on their behalf, all or part of the contract conditions (unions are a perfect example), and buyers and sellers may decide to enforce particular rules among themselves (thus company employees and outside applicants do not receive the same treatment in relation to a job vacancy in the company). A theory of the market mechanism should not only be able to deal with this multiplicity of agents and rules but also be able to explain their appearance. Nevertheless, in a good many models, the buyer and the supplier are the only economic agents likely to be present on the market, and they can form no coalitions.

2. The following question became apparent only with the beginning of research on market dynamics. The best way to introduce it is to assume that the suppliers are constantly present on the market and available to sign contracts period after period. What about the buyers then? Two extremes may be imagined:

- the buyers are also constantly present on the market and during each period endeavour to obtain the goods or services they wish to consume; in other words the set of buyers is given and these buyers' purchases are repetitive;
- the buyers enter the market in successive waves, remain present until they have completed the purchase (or purchases) they wish, then withdraw;[3] in other words, the only given is the set

---

[3] On this subject see the model by Diamond (1971).

of buyers who appear at each period (the generation of buyers) while the buyers' purchases are not repetitive.

It can be conceived that, in the first situation, the market equilibrium, if equilibrium there be, will be reached when, from period to period, each buyer buys the same quantity from the same suppliers, the state of the market reproducing itself identically from period to period, while, in the second situation, equilibrium will assume the entry, from period to period, of identical buyers, an equal flow of entries and exits, and a stationary distribution of suppliers' sales among the various generations of buyers.

3. Let us come back to the suppliers: competition analysis has long studied, in turn, the evolution of the market when no new supplier can enter the market and then when potential candidates appear. Hence a new dichotomy in the models attempting to describe the markets.

4. If we accept as given the number of sellers, the question which follows concerns the sellers' cost functions.[4] There is no need to dwell on this point since the panoply of hypotheses imaginable is well known to any economist. At one extreme can be given the quantities at the disposal of each seller, neglecting the costs or supposing that the sellers are merely retailers who have no expenses but the cost price per piece. At the other extreme one can associate with each seller an expenditure function having the usual properties assumed in micro-economic theory. But what must be emphasized is that the hypothesis made will be important to the dynamic behaviour of the market.

5. There remains one last hypothesis to introduce concerning the agents: in fact, faced with the multiplicity of problems posed by the study of the market mechanism, several writers (e.g. McMinn 1980, Reinganum 1979, and Salop and Stiglitz 1977) have limited themselves to the case in which each buyer is only interested in one unit of goods (the typical example is that of a labour-market since each job applicant only aims at holding one position during each period). When this hypothesis is assumed, one possibility is also to accept that each seller offers only one unit of goods and services.

---

[4] See particularly the models by McMinn (1980) and Reinganum (1979) in which introducing different unitary production costs among the sellers can create an equilibrium with price dispersion.

The market mechanism

It is not possible to outline here the complete typology of existing or imaginable models, but it is, nevertheless, easy to present in general terms the most fundamental questions.

1. A first consideration should be the adjustment or friction costs which intervene in the market mechanism. Reality offers an extremely wide range of such costs: from the daily trips to and from work made by an employee to the moving expenses he incurs when he must move to find a job, from the unemployment benefits a firm must pay to fire a person to the cost of training new recruits, from the psychological cost which any change of position generally represents for a person to the inconvenience most often caused a buyer by a change of suppliers. Such costs may stop the market in its dynamics and indefinitely maintain it in a state far from traditional equilibrium. A close analogy may be found with the phenomenon of heat loss through friction in thermodynamics.

2. Information is a trickier business, for, in spite of the progress of the last two decades, there is nothing to prove that economists are in any position to treat this theme fully. The difficulties are well known: if two individuals, *A* and *B*, are looking for information on an event, *E*, the behaviour of each is an indication to the other. Each one may therefore find it advantageous to modify his behaviour either to deceive or to help the other, a possibility which the other must take into account. It is therefore natural to begin by having a look at models which deal with information more simply, putting aside these subtleties—so essential to game theory. In these models, the data transmitted are exact and the agents do not worry about interpreting each other's behaviour in order to draw information from it.

3. If we take this to be true, the model-builder's first task is to specify very precisely the information which is freely available to the various categories of agent, either in the first moment or as the market is in operation. This specification may appear in the extreme form which follows: in the first moment the only information available to a buyer (seller) is that there is a seller (buyer); at the end of period *t* the only additional information available to a buyer (seller) is whether or not he has bought (sold) a unit of goods during period *t* and in case of a purchase (sale), from (to) whom and at what price. Quite often the models form other hypotheses: they take as

given that every supplier knows the demand curve or the price distribution of the set of sellers.

4. Once given the nature of the information readily available, the operation of a market results from a combination of three processes:

- a process of searching for information by the agents;
- a process of negotiation among the agents based on the information available;
- a process of revision of their anticipations and strategies by the agents.

In different cases, the descriptions of markets may bring these various processes into play simultaneously or, on the contrary, distinguish between successive phases differing in nature during which the agents collect information, negotiate, or revise their strategies. Certain models emphasize information, others negotiation, still others the revision of strategies.

5. The search for information may be described by a large variety of hypotheses. Quite often models attribute a search activity to only one category of agent, be it the buyers or the sellers.[5] As for the search itself, it may take many forms. Let us illustrate a few in the case of job hunters:

- First case: for each period, the job hunter, at no expense to himself, draws a number of positions at random. If all positions are discovered, we say that the buyer's information is extensive, but it might not be so, certain positions being unlikely to be found by the individual given his present situation and his past.
- Second case: at each period, the buyer may have knowledge of all the positions upon payment of a clearly determined price. The complete state of the market is revealed to him as soon as he pays the entrance fee.
- Third case: at each period, paying the costs of information merely gives the right to draw a sample of positions as in the first case.
- Fourth case: the individual may choose in advance the size of the sample, but the information costs to be paid in advance are an increasing (and concave) function of size.
- Fifth case: the state of each position may be revealed to the

---

[5] e.g. collecting information is uniquely an act of buyers in Diamond (1971), Fisher (1970), McMinn (1980), Reinganum (1979), Salop and Stiglitz (1977), and uniquely an act of sellers in Butters (1977).

individual in exchange for payment of information costs characteristic of the position. The individual must choose, once and for all, the positions he wants knowledge on (paying in advance the total sum of the corresponding information costs) or be authorized to proceed with a sequential search deciding at each stage whether it is worth the price to find out the conditions of such and such a position.

• Sixth case: paying information costs gives the individual the right to draw one position and the cost of information increases with the number of positions already drawn since the individual must find positions which are more and more inaccessible to him.

6. The negotiation mechanism may also be the subject of extremely varied hypotheses. In certain models of the labour-market, for example, the offers made by the sellers are steady while the buyers intervene in succession. The active buyer then compares the offers known and only (eventually) applies for one position. If the job-holder keeps his position, the buyer cannot look into another position until his next time around. He could do so in other models in which several buyers are active simultaneously. In the same manner, the existence of preferential relations between certain buyers and sellers may be an important aspect of change in the market: the homemaker goes back to the retailer who was her supplier during the previous period; a company, at equivalent price, gives priority to its former supplier.

7. The way in which the agents adjust their demands and offers also plays a role in the characterization of the models. Here we naturally run into the whole array offered by the theories on individual behaviour: at one end, an agent may be passive and content with reacting to the information communicated without building up anticipation; at the other end, he is capable of estimating the distribution of the probability of consequences in an infinite horizon and maximize a correctly defined utility. In between the two he may be content with evaluating the consequences of his acts on a horizon limited by simple procedures, thus adopting what the literature calls limited rationality behaviour. For example, a seller may be forced to express his strategy by choosing for his offer either a price level, a bottom price, or even a distribution of probability; the buyer who shows up then draws the price he is offered at random.[6]

___

[6] Price distributions for the offers chosen by the seller are for example introduced by Butters (1977).

Thus the abundance and variety of hypotheses necessary for defining a model on market dynamics explains the diversity of paths explored in the literature and the fact that only partial results are as yet available, with no synthesis of the whole to bring out a small number of general conclusions. Nevertheless, even if general results are still unavailable, the models on the dynamics of different markets already make it possible to recognize the importance of self-organization phenomena in economics and help to explore these phenomena. But to do so, one must, as always, go from the simple to the complex and begin with the detailed analysis of as elementary a model as possible. This will be the object of the following chapter.

2

A Simple Market

This chapter is devoted to the analysis of a market characterized by hypotheses as simple as possible.

1. All the actors have perfect knowledge of the goods (or service exchanged); the quality of the goods is the same for all the sellers and it remains identical throughout the evolution of the market.

2. The contracts between agents are for immediate execution and valid for only one period.

3. The buyers are of a given number, constantly present on the market, and each one desires to acquire at each period a single unit of goods (or services).

4. The sellers are of a given number and each one has at his disposal at each period one unit of goods (or services) to sell. The transaction costs are nil.

5. The sellers (or buyers) only have knowledge of their own transactions during the preceding period.

6. The search for information is made by the buyers who draw at no cost a sample of sellers at each period.

7. The price set by a seller is independent of the buyer.

This model—which will be more explicitly defined in the chapter as we go along—may be taken as representative of a labour-market but it has been designed more for conceptual ends than as a description of reality.

The chapter is divided into five sections:

- the first presents the model and a study of its dynamics;
- the second introduces the notion of surplus and brings out the significance of its evolution in time;
- the third recalls the definition of an autopoietic system and poses questions on the autopoietic nature of the preceding market;
- the last two are devoted to generalizations, the first being

limited to reinterpreting the model, while the second considers an exchange economy with any finite number of goods.

The Dynamics of a Simple Market

Continually present on this market are m workers and n positions offered by the firms. The workers are indifferent as to the positions and the firms as to the workers. Time is a discrete variable and the market mechanism operates from period to period. All wages are expressed in integers.

The individuals (represented by the letter k) are arranged in ascending order of the minimum wage demanded $\underline{w}_k$ and the positions (represented by the letter i) in descending order of the maximum wage authorized $\bar{v}_i$. $\underline{w}_k$ may be considered as the income the individual would receive if he remained unemployed and $\bar{v}_i$ as the wage above which the company would suffer a loss by filling position i.

It is assumed that the minimum wage of the Kth individual and the maximum wage of the Kth position are equal to p (Figure 2.1).

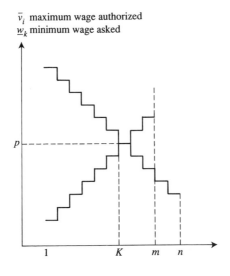

FIG. 2.1

Under these circumstances, elementary economic theory announces a single equilibrium in the market in which p is the only wage on offer while the K first individuals are employed and the K first positions filled.

Initially, all the positions are vacant and all the individuals unemployed. During a period (called a work period), certain individuals are hired (and consequently an equivalent number of positions filled), but the wages earned by the individuals generally vary since they result from independent transactions between firms and workers. If the contracts are valid for a single work period, and if the costs of a change of position for an individual and of a change of worker for a firm are nil, it will be in the firm's interest to fill the position at the lowest wage and in the worker's to obtain the highest.

In order to avoid having several candidates apply for the same position simultaneously or try to change jobs simultaneously, it is convenient to assume that the individuals show up in succession. A distinction is made between the elementary search period and the global search period. During each period of elementary search, a different individual becomes active on the market. A global search period is made up of a succession of m periods of elementary search, each individual being active one time and one time only during a global search period. It is assumed that the individuals appear in random order with uniform probability. As for the work period—the time for which a contract is signed—it may be equal to the elementary search period or to the global search period. We shall consider the first case as it is easier to present.

The first act on the part of an active individual is to seek information on the positions available through a random drawing, by means of appointments or letters of application for example, on a sample of positions. The drawing is supposedly free and the information extensive, every individual being capable of discovering every position.

The individual then considers the position (or one of the positions if there are several) which offers him the highest wage. If this wage is below his demands at the time, he will stay at his former job. If this is not the case, he will show interest in the position and there are then three possibilities:

- the position is vacant and he takes it;
- the position is held by another individual but the latter refuses the new wage and is thus replaced by the first individual;

A Simple Market   37

- the position is held by another individual who accepts the new wage and keeps his position.

The process of negotiation is extremely simple since, as we can see, given equal conditions, preference is given to the holder of the position. With time, the agents will revise their demands: an individual who does not find employment will become more conciliatory, an individual who is hired more exacting. In the same way a firm which has a position constantly filled will lower the salary proposed. There are naturally a good many ways to represent such adaptive behaviour and I shall choose the following:

- Individuals only revise their demands at the beginning of each global period. An individual without work will reduce his demands by one unit unless he has reached his minimum. An employed individual will not take another position unless he gets a wage one unit higher.

- For a position remaining vacant for two periods in a row, a firm will increase its offer if possible by one unit; for a position vacant during the last period only, it will offer the last wage paid, for a filled position it will offer wages one unit lower.

A stable state of the market is then defined as a state in which all unemployed individuals have reduced their demands to a minimum, in which all the firms with vacant positions offer a maximum wage, and in which for any one position the wage offered is inferior to the demands of all the individuals likely to find it.

It is then possible to show that, in a stable state, the first K individuals are hired and the first K positions are filled, the wages observed being limited to couples $(p-1, p)$ or $(p, p+1)$ and the states differing only in the allocation of the individuals to the positions. The existence of two possible wages in equilibrium stems from the discrete nature of the model. For elementary theory all of these stable states are obviously indistinguishable.

The following theorem is then demonstrated: given the hypotheses made, the market converges in probability towards a stable state in a finite time.[1]

Right away the reader observes an important characteristic of self-organization models: the large number of hypotheses needed for their definition. In the case of this simple model, the hypotheses

[1] It can even be shown that the mathematical expectation of the length of time at the end of which a stable state is reached is finite.

concern (as indicated in the preceding chapter) three processes and the way in which they interact:

- the process of searching for information (which concerns only individuals here);
- the process of negotiation (which brings into play in this model three factors: position, applicant, individual already holding the job);
- the process of adjusting individual and firm demands.

A whole arsenal of models can be constructed by varying the hypotheses made on these processes and the way they are linked. In the model considered here, the absence of information costs authorizes the use of rudimentary mechanisms concerning the adjustment of demands: individuals and firms do not need to deduce from market observation any expectations on the consequences of their various behaviours. They limit themselves to reacting, trying at each stage to improve their situation.

In this model, the final state of the market is independent of history, since all the stable states are indistinguishable. The processes of searching for information, negotiating, and adjusting demands simply engender an organization which separates the individuals and the positions into two groups, employed and unemployed individuals, filled and unfilled positions. There is no need, as before, for the Walras auctioneer to register offers and demands and allocate positions to individuals once the equilibrium has been calculated. The dynamics which make it possible to end up with a stable state have become endogenous.

As might be expected, necessity, chance, and will intervene simultaneously in this model.

It is the will of individuals to obtain better wages and that of enterprises to seek better profits. It is will which pushes agents into action and into keeping the evolution dynamic as long as the market is not in a stable state.

As for chance, it plays an essential role in the dynamics since it decides the order in which the individuals will show up and the positions they find. On the other hand, no event (as the word is used by Prigogine and Stengers, 1988), can possibly take place. The randomness of history has no influence whatever on the final state of the system.

Thus the system is relatively poor in self-organization properties:

it limits itself to separating individuals and firms into predetermined groups.

Lastly, necessity appears on two levels: on an elementary level through parameters which are constant in time (the $\underline{w}_k$ and the $\bar{v}_i$), on a global level since the final state of the market is foreseeable.

Among the hypotheses which are crucial to convergence towards a traditional equilibrium, two should be emphasized:

- the fact that the information is extensive, that is, any position is likely to be discovered by any individual (the next chapter will analyse what happens when this is not the case);
- the fact that, during negotiation, a firm which has not had any applicant and has a filled position agrees to keep the same individual on at the same wage, or that an employed individual who has not found a better position agrees to remain in the same position at the same wage.

What happens when the latter hypothesis is not valid?

If the firm offers any one of the individuals, including the one holding the job, wages one unit lower and/or if the individual asks of any one of the firms, including the one he is working for, wages one unit higher, there will no longer be convergence towards a state of equilibrium. Two cases are then possible:

- when at each period every individual draws a sub-set of positions which does not contain all the positions, the market fluctuates indefinitely in a random manner, wages remaining constantly dispersed;
- when at each period, every individual obtains information on the whole set of positions, the market enters at the end of a finite period of time into a sub-set of equilibria made up of states between which the market constantly fluctuates; the minimum and maximum wages observed will then be restricted by a lower and upper limit.

In these two cases, what destroys the convergence towards a stable state is the desperate attempt by the firms (and/or individuals) to reduce (or increase) the wages paid (or earned).

But let us come back to the initial model. The notion of surplus will give us a deeper understanding of its dynamics.

Surplus and its Evolution in Time

To any state of the market e_t—be it transitory or stable—we shall attach the following functions:

- the surplus $S(e_t)$ equal to the difference between the sum of the maximum wages of filled positions and the sum of the minimum wages of employed individuals;[2]
- the individual's utility, equal to the sum of a constant (his utility when unemployed) and of the difference, if employed, between his wages and his minimum $\underline{w}_k$;
- the firm's utility, equal to the sum of a constant (the utility of position i if it is vacant) and of the difference, if it is not vacant, between the maximum salary $\bar{v}_i$ and the salary paid;
- the collective utility, $v(e_t)$, the total utility of all the agents;
- the potential utility, the difference between the maximum of surplus S_M and the surplus $S(e_t)$.

We shall introduce as well the global utility, which will be the sum of collective utility and potential utility. In the system under consideration, global utility is constant as is shown by a simple calculation. The following two propositions, which constitute two ways of expressing the same results, are then easy to prove.

(i) The surplus—which is a random variable throughout the process—is maximal in a stable state and converges in probability towards this maximum in a finite amount of time.

On the other hand, the surplus does not necessarily increase during a change in the market. It may notably be at a maximum in an unstable state (it suffices to have the 'right' individual employed and the 'right' positions filled at wages different from equilibrium wages).[3]

(ii) During change in the market, global utility being constant, potential utility $(S_M - S(e_t))$ is progressively transferred to agents in

---

[2] In other words the surplus is equal to the sum over the whole set of filled positions of the differences $[\bar{v}_i - \underline{w}_{k(i)}]$, $k(i)$ being the individual who holds position i.

[3] On the other hand, by subtracting from the surplus the sum of absolute values of the differences between the wages on offer and p over the whole set of filled positions, one gets a function which is maximum in a stable state and only in a stable state. But, like the surplus, that function does not necessarily increase with a change in the market. The term subtracted in a way weighs the loss which results from price dispersion on the market.

the form of collective utility $U(e_t)$ and the potential utility is minimum in a stable state.

In other words the dynamics for the sorting of agents are also dynamics for the 'extraction of collective utility' from potential utility contained in the market. Collective utility increases along with the development of organization in the market.

Starting with a different formulation, Allais made a very pertinent study of this phenomenon in his 'Théorie générale des surplus' (1981). Working with a model similar to the one he had developed to study the general equilibrium in an economy, he introduced the notion of allocative surplus, which is equivalent, for the simple model in this chapter, to that of potential utility. Allais was right to conclude his analysis by affirming that 'in essence, all economic operations, whatever they be, may be said to come down to seeking, creating and distributing allocative surpluses'.

The similarity between change in the market and change in a gaseous thermodynamic system is obvious.[4] But several connections are possible.

In the first sense, the increase in collective utility corresponds in thermodynamics to a decrease in entropy, the decrease in potential utility to an increase in useful energy. As for global utility it plays the role of internal energy. Its constance is an energy-saving relation. In comparison to the vocabulary of thermodynamics, one may say that when this relation is proven, the dynamics of the market are reversible dynamics which engender no loss of global utility, but may be expressed, on the other hand, by a supplement of organization due to the association of firms and workers.

Nevertheless, the reversibility resulting from the absence of friction does not exclude an irreversible change in the system from pressure exerted by the actors' individual will, since, for the latter, collective utility and potential utility are obviously not equivalent. Hence a second interpretation which associates surplus and entropy and considers that the evolution of the market towards equilibrium is comparable to the homogenization of the temperature of a gas. From this point of view, the dynamics of the market destroy the initial organization which separates firms from workers. But, unlike the physicist, the economist does not deem it useful to emphasize this form of disorganization. He therefore judges the spontaneous

---

[4] See the detailed analyses by Denniel (1989) on this subject.

market dynamics as described in this chapter, as conserving global utility, generating a surplus, and creating an order.

It thus appears that the term irreversibility may be the object of two different definitions. To avoid any ambiguity, throughout the remainder of the book, I shall take the term to mean any evolution which does not conserve global utility.

The preceding remarks make it possible to question the efficiency of the market as a resource allocation process. If the agents have neither information costs nor adjustment costs and if the discount coefficients of their utilities are equal to 1, the limit, when t increases indefinitely, of the quotient of the sum of the agents' utilities over the first t periods of time divided by t is equal to the maximum collective utility. In other words, the market in this case may be seen as a process of perfect allocation. This property results from the fact that the mathematical expectation on the time period at the end of which the market is in a stable state is finite. But in practice loss is caused by three things:

1. Individuals, in their search for positions, and firms, in giving information on those positions, must bear expenses which have to be deducted from the utility of each period.

2. For individuals to change jobs and for firms to change job holders, they must bear costs which reduce the utility of each period.

3. Agents discount their future utilities. And until the random time T when stability is reached, collective utility is below its maximum.

As we shall see later on, the causes of loss modify market dynamics, but, leaving this aspect aside for a moment, we can define as operational loss the difference between the present value of collective utility, when the maximum of that utility is attained as early as the first period, and the mathematical expectation of the present value of the utility on the set of changes possible from the first moment on. In other words, the economic agents have to pay something for extracting collective utility from potential utility. Under these circumstances, it is permissible to say that the real market is a process of imperfect allocation.

Introducing surpluses already throws light on the concept of self-organization, but the reference to autopoiesis will help us along with our analysis.

The Market as an Autopoietic System

Within the last ten years, numerous authors have become interested in autopoietic systems, that is to say, systems capable of producing themselves. Milan Zeleny gives the following description: 'An autopoietic system is a distinguishable complex of component-producing processes and their resulting components, bounded as an autonomous unity within its environment and characterized by a particular kind of relations among its components and component-producing processes: the components through their interaction, recursively generate, maintain and recover the same complex of processes which produced them' (Zeleny 1980).

An autopoietic system thus assumes:

- production processes which assure the synthesis, transformation, or disintegration of the components;
- an organization made up of an invariable set of relations between components and processes;
- a closed organization, each process necessarily dependent on the others for its creation and maintenance.

The authors who introduced the concepts consider autopoiesis to be a property characteristic of living organisms. They often furnish as an example of an autopoietic system, a model of a cell in which the components can occupy all the co-ordinate points on a two-dimensional plane. The components may be the following:

- a catalyst x;
- a substratum y;
- an element without links u;
- an element with one link v;
- an element with two links w;
- a hole (a vertex without any of the components).

Initially all the vertices are filled with substratum, except for one central one which receives a catalyst. Then three types of processes and rules of movement come into play. The processes intervene between adjacent components. They are:

- a process of production:
  $2y + x \Rightarrow u + x + $ (hole)
  (an element without links is obtained from a substratum);

- a process of linkage:

  $v - w - \ldots - v + u \Rightarrow v - w - \ldots - w - v$

  (an element without links enters into a linkage made up of elements having two links with an element having one link at each end);
- processes of disintegration:

  $u + (\text{hole}) \Rightarrow 2y$

  $v + (\text{hole}) \Rightarrow 2y$

  $w + (\text{hole}) \Rightarrow 2y$

Obviously these processes form a closed organization.

As for the rules of movement, they allow a catalyst, for example, to displace units without links or substratum into adjacent holes or to change positions with them. All the movements, productions, linkages, and disintegrations are determined in a random manner. We then witness, if the probabilities of disintegration are not too high, the formation of a closed linkage of adjacent w components surrounding the catalyst and consequently separating the elements inside the cell from those without.

Figure 2.2 (borrowed from Zeleny 1980) reproduces, in a lexico-graphic order, several steps of a simulation putting into evidence the progressive and random emergence of a closed boundary of the cell. The fundamental question posed is then the following: does the market such as it has been described in this chapter form an autopoietic system? To furnish an answer to that question, we must identify the components and the processes, to show that they make up an organization and to bring out the closed nature of that organization.

In the model presented, three categories of components exist: isolated individuals, vacant positions, and couples of a filled position and an employed individual.

An individual component is characterized by two series of attributes: the individual's minimum wage, $\underline{w}_k$, and his wage demands. In the same way a position component is characterized by the maximum wage $\bar{v}_i$ and the one offered. Lastly, a couple component brings in four series of attributes (the permanent characteristics and the demands of the firms and the employees).

Three types of processes have been introduced, but they must be reinterpreted if we are to understand their role in autopoiesis:

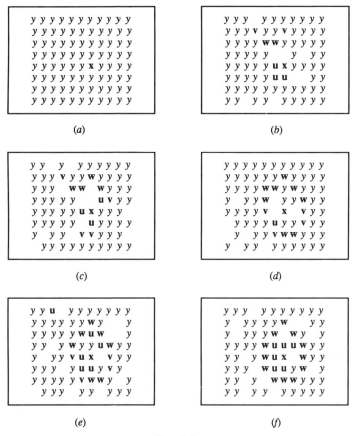

Fig. 2.2

- the information search process brings an isolated or employed individual from a couple into contact with a sub-set of other position components or position–individual couples;
- the negotiation process fulfils a triple function: the selection of a component from the sub-set discovered; the eventual destruction of couple components during the negotiation; the creation of a new couple component;
- finally, the demand adjustment process modifies the variable attributes of the components by changing the salaries offered or asked, but not just any modifications take place: satisfied

demands tend to be reinforced and unsatisfied demands to be weakened.

The relations between the processes and the components may be described by bringing in only the state of the system or random drawings. They are then invariable and consequently constitute an organization.

Is this organization a closed one? For this to be the case, each process must necessarily depend on the others for its realization and maintenance.

Let us begin with the process of searching for information. It starts at each period only after the demands have been adjusted and after the individuals' order of appearance has been drawn at random. As for the negotiation process, it can be opened only after agents have been brought together. At the beginning of the market history, it is limited to generating links between two agents, the couples, then, as time goes on, it dissociates existing links in order to build new ones. Nevertheless, the links constructed become stronger and stronger as the market nears stability, until finally the process of demand adjustment only appears once the preceding reallocations are completed. The circular nature of the linkage of the three processes ensures the closing of the organization on itself.

It is therefore not surprising to find far-reaching analogies between this dynamic model of a market and the model proposed above to describe the formation of a cell.

In the case of the market, the forming of the membrane is represented by the separation into two groups of individuals (those who are employed and those who are not) and of positions (those which are filled and those which are not). Agents may be said to be 'in' or 'out' of the market. There is thus no doubt that the market described in this chapter may be considered an autopoietic system. This observation leads us to take a new look at certain properties of the model.

The traditional economist has become accustomed to considering economic equilibrium as a state which reproduces itself identically from period to period. But there is nothing of that here, because, even if the salary operating remains constant and even if the jobs of the individuals are not modified, the latter continue a permanent search for information. In other words, the system maintains itself in a state of alertness, and it is only because the individuals never discover an interesting position that the chain of processes is not set to work.

But if exogenous shocks take place (the modification of $\bar{v}_i$ or $\underline{w}_k$, the arrival or departure of individuals, the creation or disappearance of enterprises), new dynamics may be set in motion. As the market ends up in a stable state in an uncertain, finite period of time, it is capable on average of re-establishing its equilibrium if the shocks are infrequent and of limited size. Still, as disturbances increase, the market has less and less time to adjust and the average departure from equilibrium (measured, for example, by the salary dispersion operating in relation to the equilibrium salary) increases until the market has lost all capacity for autopoiesis.

It stands to reason that the resilience of the market depends on the behaviour of individuals, notably:

- the size of the average sample drawn during the search process;
- the rapidity of demand adjustment.

One may imagine, for example, that if the individuals' information is improved, and they make better use of that information to modify their demands more rapidly, market resilience in relation to exogenous shocks will increase. On the other hand, it can be shown that this is not necessarily the case when the increase in the size of the sample engenders no change in the demand adjustment process. Everything happens then as if the change in the latter were disturbed by an excess of information. From that point on, the average convergence time may increase.

It thus seems clear that market analysis in terms of self-organization deeply modifies the vision one might have of its operations. Under these circumstances, one question naturally comes to mind: can the foregoing model be generalized for any sort of exchange economy with m individuals and n goods? The analysis of that question will be the subject of the last part of this chapter, but first we shall introduce a variant of the model which is interesting in itself.

A Model Variant

In this variant, the only agents on the market will be individuals k, m in numbers ($1 \leq k \leq m$). During each period every individual will practise one of the following three activities: craftsman, entrepreneur, employee.

If he is a craftsman he will work alone and will receive $\underline{w}_k$ as a remuneration.

If he is an entrepreneur he will necessarily take on an employee and ensure himself a net income of $\bar{v}_k - s_k$, $\bar{v}_k$ standing for his gross income and s_k for the salary he pays his employee.

If he is an employee he will necessarily work for an entrepreneur and consequently receive the salary this entrepreneur pays him.

To simplify matters, it is accepted that individuals may vary as to their professional skills as craftsmen or entrepreneurs but are interchangeable as employees.

At the outset, all the individuals are craftsmen, but while staying in contact with each other, they will try to find out whether it is advantageous for them to become entrepreneurs or employees.

In that case, during each period (called a work period) a certain number of individuals will become salaried (and consequently an equal number of individuals will become entrepreneurs) but the salaries earned will generally be different since they result from independent transactions between entrepreneurs and workers. It will be in the entrepreneur's interest to fill the position at the lowest salary and in the worker's interest to try to get the highest. All the same, the entrepreneur and the worker will wonder if it would not be in their interest to change activities.

Except for these few adaptations, the model is constructed like the one presented in the course of this chapter. A stable state is defined as a state: (1) in which all the craftsmen have reduced to a minimum their demands as salaried workers and raised to a maximum their offer as an entrepreneur; (2) in which for every existing or potential position, the salary offered is inferior to the demands of all the individuals likely to discover it; (3) in which every entrepreneur or worker has a revenue as high or higher than the one he would have as a craftsman.

Naturally, as for the initial model, the market converges in probability towards a stable state in a finite time. But how can stable states be characterized a priori? It can be done approximately by starting with Fig. 2.3 in which each individual may be localized by his co-ordinates $(\underline{w}_k, \bar{v}_k)$. Let it be accepted for simplicity's sake that we are in the presence of a continuous distribution of individuals $f(\underline{w}, \bar{v})$, on the first quadrant, and let us seek out all the states in which all the workers are occupied at salary s.

An individual is then:

- a craftsman if $\underline{w}_k \leq s$ and $\underline{w}_k > \bar{v}_k - s$
- a worker if $\underline{w}_k < s$ and $s > \bar{v}_k - s$
- an entrepreneur if $\underline{w}_k < \bar{v}_k - s$ and $s < \bar{v}_k - s$

Consequently, if in Figure 2.3, for a given value of s, lines $w = s$, $v = w + s$, $v = 2s$ are drawn:

- the workers occupy the rectangle *Obcd*;
- the craftsmen occupy the polygon situated to the right of the contour *bce*;
- the entrepreneurs occupy the polygon situated above the contour *dce*.

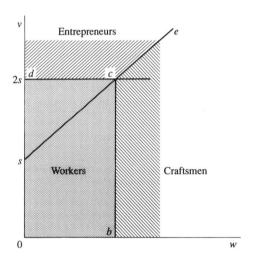

Fig. 2.3

As can easily be seen, when s increases, redrawing the straight lines increases the number of workers and reduces the number of entrepreneurs. As $\bar{v}$ is bounded by the value V and $0 \leq s \leq V$, it results in the existence of one value s^* and only one for which the number of entrepreneurs is equal to the number of workers.

It may be shown that the states of the market thus defined are the stable states of the processes previously described. With one slight exception: as a result of the discrete nature of the model, one can find salary couples $(s^*, s^* - 1)$ or $(s^*, s^* + 1)$ instead of the single salary s^*.

From a formal point of view, this model is simply a reinterpretation of the starting model, but its economic significance is considerable since the market determines the roles of individuals in society. Starting with undifferentiated individuals—with disorder therefore —it progressively separates the individuals through a random process into craftsmen, entrepreneurs, and employees. It therefore engenders order, the construction of that order going hand in hand with the elaboration of a single salary.

An Exchange Economy

It is reasonable to wonder if the ideas underlying the model in this chapter can be applied to an exchange economy with an undetermined number of goods. The work of Lainé (1987, 1989) confirms an answer in the affirmative but also emphasizes the depth of the field left to be explored. Indeed, his work is limited to a sequential economy of bilateral exchanges without seeking to explain why, based only on individuals' behaviour, transactions are limited to this type.

Summarily described, the Lainé model is given below.

$I = \{1, \ldots, i, \ldots, n\}$ and $M = \{1, \ldots, 1, \ldots, m\}$ denote respectively the set of agents and the set of goods ($n, m < \infty$). The set of what agent i consumes is supposedly equal to R^m_+ and his preferences are represented by a complete pre-order R_i defined on R^m_+. Technical assumptions ensure that individual preferences have the 'good' properties generally postulated by literature.

An allocation is defined as a vector $\mathbf{x} = (x_i)i \notin I$. The initial resource allocation will be denoted by $\mathbf{w} = (w_i)i \notin I$ and the set of realizable allocations (i.e. such that for every commodity i, the sum of individual consumptions, does not exceed the available amount w_i) will be represented by $A(w)$.

At each date t, a pair of agents, who decide to carry out a set of transactions, is formed thus determining the situation of the economy that prevails before the exchanges of date ($t + 1$). The succession of bilateral contacts is represented by a series of transpositions $(\pi^t)_{t \in N}$ on $I(\pi^t(i) = j$ meaning that the pair $\{i, j\}$ is formed at date t).

The pair $\{i, j\}$ being formed, one of the two agents is chosen at random as leader and the one responsible for proposing the prices which will be applied during the exchange. It is accepted that the leader is perfectly informed on the behaviour of his colleague and that the passive agent does not waver in his strategy; his only reaction consists in proposing:

- either the transactions which allow him to maximize his utility in the budgetary set imposed by the leader if they improve the situation that he had before the exchange;
- or the status quo if every transaction at the imposed prices worsens his initial situation.

The leader then chooses the price system which maximizes his own utility, considering the reaction, that is to say, the other agent's exchange proposition.

This negotiation procedure defines a monotonous exchange process—that is to say, a process which guarantees a non-decreasing agent utility at each date. As Lainé (1989) writes, this procedure is undeniably very primitive:

if in a situation of unequal information distribution, the establishment of a Stackelberg equilibrium may seem probable in a game where the players only play once, the repetition of the game and the acquisition of information on the others' strategies which it permits, can only incite the passive agent to manipulate the leaders' decisions to his own advantage, for example by deforming his preferences or lying about the state of his endowment. In as much as, here, we are putting aside all dynamic interaction between successive negotiations, the change in the market results from the superimposing of totally myopic and amnesic strategies. Furthermore, no description is offered of the means of selecting a leader.

The sequential process P which has just been introduced associates with each series $\{\pi^t\}_t$ a corresponding set of allocation trajectories $\{x^t\}_t$ and a set of price trajectories $\{p^t\}_t$. We shall call an associate trajectory of P any series $\{p^t, x^t\}_t$ such that $x_0 = w$ and $x^{t+1} \in \Omega(x_t)$, Ω designating the set of these allocations likely to result from the bilateral exchanges at any date.

The object of the analysis is obviously the study of P's asymptotic behaviour. To come up with significant results, adequate regularity must be imposed following the contact between agents. Hence the introduction of the following definition.

The series $\{\pi^t\}_t$ of transpositions of pairs of agents is said to be regular if it constitutes an *ad infinitum* succession of cycles of the same finite length such that within each one every pair of agents is formed at least once.

The notion of regularity evidently plays the same role here as extensive information plays in the simple model seen in this chapter. With the preceding hypotheses, the following theorem can be demonstrated.

If $(\pi')_t$ is regular and within the hypotheses drawn up on individual preferences, the process P leads to a Pareto-type resource distribution and every trajectory $\{p_t, x_t\}$ associated with P converges towards a price equilibrium (p, x).[5]

There naturally exist a priori several accessible price equilibria and their characterization remains an open question.

Such results represent an important step towards a satisfactory modelling of the operation of a self-organizing market economy. Its importance lies in showing that a succession of bilateral negotiations, mutually independent (and therefore having a priori very different prices from period to period) may lead the market towards an efficient situation in which a perfectly unified price system prevails which no agent is likely to question.

Nevertheless, the preceding process gives a very rudimentary representation of the self-organized market. Different possibilities for enriching the model are conceivable.

A first question concerns the way pairs are formed. The advantage of an approach which takes the contact process to be totally exogenous lies in showing the importance of adequate conditions of regularity in pair formation for obtaining stable exchange trajectories. One possible way is to introduce a random contact mechanism and to assume that, as in the simple model, the probability that such and such a pair be drawn at a particular date is strictly positive. However, 'if such a procedure may constitute a correct approximation of reality when there is a large number of agents, it seems more difficult to justify when there are relatively few: unless it can be assumed that acquiring information on the others is quite costly, one can in fact estimate that at the end of an initial period of experimentation each agent is in a position to establish at date t a pre-order of preference on the set of pairs he may help to form' (Lainé 1989).

---

[5] It is called a price equilibrium when a couple (p, x) is such that for every i, x_i maximizes the utility of agent i in the budget set defined by px_i.

Even so it results in only a limited enrichment of the initial model. First of all, because no description is made of the partner-seeking mechanism in relation to the pre-order of preferences. Secondly, because 'if the criteria for individual agent classification may be upheld in the case of a Stackelberg type of exchange procedure where the leader is drawn at random, it becomes much less interesting if the negotiation procedure is enriched in such a way that permanently myopic and amnesic conduct be replaced by aspects more in line with the sequential nature of contacts' (Lainé 1989). Lastly, because it has been assumed to start with that only bilateral transactions are possible when explanation should be given as to why such transactions are more probable than those involving several agents.

The spectrum of possibilities is also quite large as concerns the negotiation procedure set in motion at each date. It all depends on how the agents' attitude towards time and their computation possibilities are taken into account.

One end of the spectrum (the one we are interested in) corresponds to a case of perfectly myopic rules of decision: change in the market is then governed by a succession of partial negotiations founded only on blind consideration of the present and led by agents with a total inaptitude for retaining history lessons. At the other end of the spectrum, are the beginnings of a situation in which each agent draws up a behaviour strategy beforehand which he has merely to follow from step to step. The organization of the market is then described with the help of a non-cooperative game in extended form; evidently, the negotiation procedure, though it remains to be specified, becomes dependent on prior decisions, which themselves, given the complexity and diversity of the possible situations to be grasped before the opening of the market, rest upon the considerable number of computation possibilities.

The most satisfactory formalization is no doubt intermediary: it cannot reduce individual behaviour to prior elaboration of a single strategy nor to the succession of mutually dependent punctual decisions. It must be able to define the mechanisms according to which the agents acquire, period after period, better knowledge of exchange opportunities, eventually forget the distant past, extract learning from past negotiations, and anticipate future market situations, thus conforming to a strategy which is itself sequential and of which the principles may be quite complex. (Lainé 1989)

These commentaries make it possible to envisage the extent of research to be carried on. They also suggest two conjectures which may usefully serve as conclusions to this chapter:

1. It seems probable, first of all, assuming that all agents may participate in exchanges, that a large range of sequential exchange processes are likely to lead to convergence towards a price equilibrium. In other words, the market appears to be an extremely robust self-organization mechanism. It works just as well with agents having complex strategies as with actors having simple rules for decision-making. It would be interesting in this respect to know whether it is possible to define a sort of classification for sequential exchange processes and to characterize the 'minimal processes' necessarily leading to a unique single system of price equilibrium.

2. In the second place, it seems likely that, inasmuch as there exist several equilibria in an exchange economy,[6] the agents' strategies and the effects of random events inherent in the processes have an influence on the equilibrium which is attained. From this point of view, the market could reveal itself to be extremely sensitive to individual behaviour, the stable state which comes into being depending—even in the absence of irreversibilities—on the development and the computational capacity of the agents. Here there is obviously a research theme of the greatest interest.

Phenomena which are analogous but engendered by the existence of irreversibilities will be brought out in the next chapter.

---

[6] Contrary to the case of the simple model.

3

The Market and Irreversibilities

If the simple market in the last chapter necessarily converges towards the traditional equilibrium, it is because its operation engenders no costs: the individuals draw their job samples free of charge and can discover any job whatsoever; they can change jobs without having the least expense to bear while the firms can replace one worker with another without having to experience the least loss. It is an ideal world far removed from reality.

As a result, however, one cannot help but wonder what happens to the dynamics of a market when irreversibilities are taken into account. To furnish an answer to that question is the aim of this chapter, a chapter which will permit the introduction of several notions of importance for all that follows in the book.

Three situations will be examined in turn:

• In the first, the jobs which an individual can discover or hold are functions of the job he already holds (for example, a fitter from Citroën will only have access to jobs offered by the automobile industry); in other words, every individual can no longer be an applicant at any time whatsoever for any job whatsoever on the market: the set of his possibilities is a function of his present job.

• In the second situation, the economic agents must bear the costs of transition. These costs will be introduced into two different contexts: (1) where there exists as in the preceding chapter only one labour-market, but the companies cannot fire an individual or individuals change jobs without sustaining losses (monetary or psychological); (2) where there exist several labour-markets situated in different localities, but where an individual has to move in order to gain access to jobs in localities other than the one he lives in.

• In the third situation, individuals can only draw a job sample in exchange for more or less substantial information costs and their chances depend on their propensity for being spontaneously active on the market.

Except for these few modifications imposed by the situation, the models examined will be the same as the one analysed in Chapter 2.

The Model with Access Structured by Positions

In this model, with every position i ($0 \le i \le n$, $i = 0$ designating by convention the situation of unemployment) may be associated a set L_i of jobs accessible during period ($t + 1$) to the individual who holds job i at period t. In other terms, when individual k, who is employed at job $i_t(k)$ during period t, becomes active on the market, it is from $L_{i_t(k)}$ that he draws the sample of jobs to consider.

With this new hypothesis, the market always converges in probability towards a stable state, but the stable states can no longer be reduced to a traditional equilibrium (even if this equilibrium is naturally part of them). In particular, there appear stable states having the following two properties:

- the first K individuals are not all employed and/or the first K positions are not all filled, contrary to what happens in extensive information;
- the salaries paid on the market may differ by more than 1; in other words a stability with price dispersion is conceivable.

Hence we are brought to define three properties of stable states and to study the conditions necessary and sufficient under which stable states would possess these properties:

- a stable state is said to be efficient if, in that state, the first K individuals are employed and the first K jobs filled—that is to say, if it does the same sorting as the market in the preceding chapter;
- a stable state is said to be concentrated if, in that state, the salaries paid do not differ by more than 1—that is to say, there is but one single equilibrium salary;
- a stable state is said to be perfect if it is both concentrated and efficient; it then corresponds to a traditional equilibrium.

These conditions are only verified exceptionally, and consequently, when access is structured by employment, the set of stable states includes both stable states corresponding to the traditional equilibrium and other stable states.

If we consider, then, that two stable states in which the same individuals are employed and the same positions filled are indistinguishable and correspond to the same condensed state of the market, we observe:

- that a given condensed stable state cannot be reached from just any initial state of the market;
- that several condensed stable states may on the other hand be reached from the same initial state.

Therefore, when access barriers exist, the initial state, the order of appearance of individuals on the market, and the samples they draw during their search have an influence on the stable state which is established. The mark of time has reappeared, the market has a history.

As for surplus, it can be shown to be locally maximum in any stable state (though the opposite is not true). One can then associate four notions with each initial state:

- the maximum surplus one can hope to obtain from this state;
- the coefficient of efficiency, the ratio of the maximum surplus likely to be attained to the 'maximum maximorum' surplus;
- the mathematical expectation of surplus obtained when the market has attained stability;[1]
- the coefficient of average efficiency, the ratio of this mathematical expectation to the maximum maximorum surplus.

As a result of its historical change, it is possible for the market to be trapped in a stable state, which may be an unsatisfactory one. Figure 3.1 gives an intuitive explanation of how this problem arises. Let us suppose that the dynamics of the market can lead only to two condensed stable states g_1 and g_2, g_1 corresponding to a traditional equilibrium. Certain states of the market like g_3 are such that starting from there dynamic change may lead to g_1 or g_2. On the contrary, others like g_4 or g_5 may be such that change will necessarily lead to g_1 only or g_2 only. In other terms, g_4 is in the field of

---

[1] For each stable state which can be reached from the initial state considered, one weights the corresponding surplus by the probability of that state and one sums up the products obtained on the set of stable states (for a given initial state the probability attached to any stable state is well defined since the evolution of the market is governed by a Markov process).

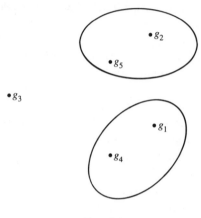

FIG. 3.1

attraction—the trap of g_1—while g_5 is in the g_2 trap. These two traps are forcibly disjointed sets, and each one has a boundary such that, if the market crosses it, it is ineluctably attracted by g_1 or by g_2. The study of the boundaries of the traps does not lead to results simple enough to be presented here.

Here then we are in the presence of a first model in which the history of the market leads to multiple equilibria. The origin of the phenomenon is, here, the existence of constraints where access to jobs is concerned. But this form of friction is hardly creative since it keeps the market from drawing a maximum from the surplus and in so doing generates an economic loss.

The Model with Transition Costs

The two situations which are to be considered here correspond first to the simple existence of friction costs, and secondly to a geographic dispersion of the labour-markets.

Existence of friction costs

The model in Chapter 2 will be retained with only two exceptions:

• With each position $i(1 \leq i \leq n)$ will be associated a cost $c_i \geq 1$ such that if the position is filled, the company will offer the new applicant not the salary paid lowered by one unit, but the salary paid lowered by c_i; in fact, the firm supposedly bears, in the case of a change of job-holder, a cost $(c_i - 1)$ representing the expense of firing the former job-holder, the expense of training the new applicant, and the psychological cost of change.

• With each individual $k(1 \leq k \leq m)$ will be associated a cost $d_k \geq 0$ such that, if the individual is employed, he will only accept a new job if his salary rises by $d_k + 1$; in fact, the individual supposedly has to pay, in case of a change of jobs, a sum d_k representing the monetary and psychological cost of his readjustment.

The reader will immediately notice that this representation of friction costs is arbitrary: it is over the whole length of time the new worker holds down the job and not only on the next period that the firm hopes to save more than c_i; it is on the length of his next employment and not only on the next period that the individual hopes to receive a supplement of income superior to d_k. In other words, as soon as friction costs enter the picture, it becomes strictly necessary to bring in agents' expectations. This is what we shall do in the next section when considering information costs, but, for the moment, we shall limit ourselves to a simpler representation of behaviour.

It is easy to show that in the model in which the agents limit themselves to considering their immediate advantages, introducing friction costs enlarges the set of stable states and brings out stable states distinct from traditional equilibrium. More precisely, the stable states may be divided into three sub-sets:

• a sub-set of efficient states of which all may not be concentrated;
• a sub-set of states in which the first K individuals are employed, but in which some of the first K jobs are vacant;
• a sub-set in which the first K positions are filled but in which some of the first K individuals are jobless.

As for salary dispersion in a stable state, dispersion measured by the difference of the highest and the lowest salaries on the market, it is possible to fix an upper limit. This limit brings in the sums $(c_i + d_k)$ which one can associate in a market state with each job plus job-holder couple (i, k). Analysis thus confirms that, the higher the friction costs, the greater the range of possible wage dispersion.

In terms of collective utility, a stable state e is now characterized by the fact that for each state e' which may be reached from e, the difference in collective utility $Ue' - U_e$ is inferior to friction costs which agents bear when going from e to e'. One can also modify the definitions of agents' utilities and consider the variation of utility from e to e' including as a negative term the friction costs he bears. With these new definitions, the variation of collective utility is negative for every passage from a stable state e to another state e'.

Therefore, the existence of friction costs implies that the market may, depending on its history, be trapped in states in which the sorting out of individuals (and jobs) is only imperfectly carried out and in which the constructing of a single price is not completed.

Presence of geographically dispersed employment markets

The work positions are now geographically dispersed among L different localities. Individuals must reside in the locality where they work. They nevertheless have the possibility of moving from one locality to another in order to gain access to new positions.

To describe this situation, the usual theory of migrations assumes that an individual compares the present value of his future net income with or without a move, which assumes that he is capable of solving one of the most complex dynamic problems! Thus we have judged it more realistic to form the hypothesis that an individual, living in one locality and planning on moving to another, directly compares the salaries offered him with an anticipated cost of access associated with moving from the first locality to the second. Such a cost includes not only the monetary and psychological cost of the move but also the values each individual attaches to his future job prospects and salaries in each case.

A state in an economy is now characterized by a geographic distribution of individuals and by the assigning of individuals to positions (including unemployment). All other things being equal, the existence of anticipated costs of access naturally engenders a loss of collective utility when individuals' geographic distribution is modified.

One is thus led to introduce two optimum state concepts for the set of markets:

1. A state is a local optimum, if there does not exist any change from that state which engenders an increase of collective utility.

2. A state is a differential optimum in relation to an initial state if, considering the anticipated access costs, the increase of collective utility associated with such a change is equal or superior to that associated with every other change from the initial state.

These definitions imply that a differential optimum is a local optimum but that the contrary is generally not true. Under these circumstances, if two notions of optimality may be introduced, an obvious question for the economist is whether there exist two notions of stability associated with them. The answer is affirmative:

1. The first notion is that of local stability: a state is locally stable if, for every individual, his salary in that state is superior to the one he is offered for every other position, once the anticipated access cost if necessary has been deducted. It is possible to demonstrate the equivalence between the set of local optima and that of locally stable states.
2. The second notion is that of differential stability: a state is differentially stable in relation to an initial state if it is not refused by any individual or by any coalition of an individual and a position, considering the states that these coalitions may be assured of attaining from the initial state. It is possible to demonstrate the equivalence between the set of differential optima and that of differentially stable states.

The dynamic processes described in the preceding chapter ensure, from any initial state, the convergence in probability of the set of markets towards a locally stable state, but nothing guarantees that this state is differentially stable in relation to the initial state.

Why is that? A simple example makes it immediately understandable. Let us suppose that the differential optimum implies that individual k_1, initially unemployed, and residing in $l(k_1)$ takes position i_1 located in $L(i_1)$. It may be that firm i_1 will, at that period, make an offer $s(i_1)$ too low to be of interest to individual k_1:

$$s(i_1) - \underline{w}(k_1) - d\,[l(k_1), L(i_1)] \leq 0 \qquad (1)$$

$d[l(k_1), L(i_1)]$ designating the anticipated access cost of $l(k_1)$ at $L(i_1)$. The individual may then accept the offer of another firm and move to i_2. But once in i_2, the i_1 offer may never become interesting because:

$$\bar{v}(i_1) - \bar{v}(i_2) - d[L(i_2), L(i_1)] \leq 0 \tag{2}$$

Individual k_1 may then be trapped in a locally stable state.

This could not have been the case, if individual k_1 and firm i_1 had formed a coalition to refuse any move which did not procure them at least:

$$\bar{v}(i_1) - \underline{w}(k_1) - d[l(k_1), L(i_1)]$$

This result illustrates a very important trait of geographic change in an economy: the spatial distribution of individuals is not predetermined; it results from the history of market adjustment and from an initial state. The transition costs may lock an economy into a state very different from the differential optimum. In fact, when an individual moves to bring in immediate earnings higher than his anticipated access cost, he may keep the market from later reaching the differential optimum. It is the notion of differential stability which characterizes the level of co-operation between the agents necessary to avoid this disadvantage. In reality, the absence of co-operation among the agents engenders a distribution of economic activities which is only locally optimal, the agents having to withstand, for example, costs of congestion.

The existence of anticipated access costs is obviously not the only source of self-organization in geographic economics. Two other phenomena play an essential role as the work of the Prigogine school has well demonstrated: economies of scale and links between the various economic activities. But these problems will not be treated in this volume.

The Model with Information Costs

The introduction of information costs (Laffond and Lesourne 1981, 1985) profoundly modifies the market dynamics for three main reasons:

1. The individuals must now decide whether or not it is preferable to bear the information costs in order to obtain employment. They

must consequently estimate their salary prospects if they begin to job hunt. There is no question of their limiting themselves to reacting to the propositions received. An expectation is necessary, even within the framework of behaviour of limited rationality.

2. The individuals are interested in discovering the positions for two different reasons: actually to be applicants, or to be informed on the market situation in order to decide whether or not to search.

3. The relations between a job and the individual who holds it become more crucial than before: indeed, in his evaluation of the situation, an individual is brought to consider the presence or absence of privileged ties with his present employer. The existence of such ties is necessary in order for the process to converge towards a stable state.

To take into account these different aspects, the model in Chapter 2 must be modified. We shall proceed with a brief description of the transformations which would have to be made, then interpret the results.

Description of the model

During period t, individuals attempt to sign work contracts for period $(t + 1)$. Their search is carried out in two sub-periods. During the first sub-period, a privileged tie exists between a job and the job-holder; this tie is broken during the second sub-period, and the market is then said to be 'free'.

At the beginning of the first sub-period, each individual (as a consequence of the past) knows of a sub-set of jobs, and, if he is employed, his present job. On the other hand, each firm has announced the wage it is offering during period $(t + 1)$.

The individuals then enter the market one after another, each only once, and in random order. They go to see about each job that they know of, and apply for the best job they find if it is interesting. If the job is taken, the holder has the right of pre-emption at the wage offered, on condition that he has not yet been present on the market. The job is given to the first applicant or the job-holder and the contract is firm for period $(t + 1)$. There is only one exception: if the firm has not yet found an applicant when the job-holder enters the market, it offers him for $(t + 1)$ the same wage as in period t (the hypothesis is essential for convergence to a stable state).

During the second sub-period, four categories of agent, with different motivations, operate on the market:

- individuals who have found a job for $(t + 1)$ are limited to seeking information on the market and to registering themselves for the sub-sets of jobs they will consider during the first sub-period of $(t + 1)$ in order to find employment for $(t + 2)$;
- individuals who have not yet found a job for $(t + 1)$ add to the preceding motivations the desire to find employment for $(t + 1)$;
- firms whose positions are filled for $(t + 1)$ seek only to register individuals as potential applicants of the first sub-period of $(t + 1)$;
- firms whose positions are still vacant in $(t + 1)$ want in addition to find job-holders for that period.

The firms in the first category have therefore only one wage offer to make (for period $(t + 2)$), while those in the second category must propose a wage for $(t + 1)$ and a wage for $(t + 2)$.

During this second sub-period, the individuals enter the market one after the other, each only once, and in random order. An individual $k(1 \leq k \leq m)$ then draws a sample of firms, finds out the wage offer (or offers) made, and decides according to his situation:

- if he is an applicant for a job for $(t + 1)$, and if so which one;
- if he will register with a firm for consideration during the first sub-period of $(t + 1)$.

Every applicant to be registered is accepted and the first applicant for an available position for the period $(t + 1)$ gets the position at the salary offered.

In such a model, there may be four types of information costs:

- the search costs borne by the individuals when they draw a sample of jobs in the second sub-period (these costs may be connected with the drawing itself or be a function of the number of jobs drawn—logically the individuals could moreover reconsider their decision after drawing each job);
- the costs of enrolment which must be paid by the individual when he enrols for a job during the second sub-period (these costs may be connected with the act of enrolment itself or may be a function of the number of jobs retained);
- costs of application which are paid by an individual when he applies for a job in the first or second sub-period; these costs

cover not only the transmitting of a piece of information to a company (letter of application or appointment) but also the eventual psychological trauma of an irreversible decision;

- costs of updating the lists which are borne during the first sub-period by the individual who enters the market and who must gather information on the list of jobs still available in the set of those for which he enrolled.

It can be shown that with hypotheses on negotiation and demand adjustment close to those in Chapter 2, the market converges in probability in finite time to a traditional equilibrium when all the information costs above are nul. But what is the case when these costs are not nul?

I shall limit myself here to a case in which there is a fixed research cost to be paid by an individual for the right to draw on a sample.

The basic problem is describing an individual's behaviour. This behaviour concerns the observation of the market, the act of application, and the adaptation of expectations. With regard to observation, one of the possible ways of describing individual behaviour consists of assuming that at the beginning of the second sub-period of period t, the individual makes five estimations:

- the first is the value he attaches to immediate observation of the market;
- the second (and respectively the third) is the value he attaches to the observation of the market during period $(t + 1)$ if the market has not been observed during period t (and respectively, if the market has been observed during period t);
- the fourth is the salary he hopes to get for period $(t + 1)$ if he seeks employment for that period during the second sub-period of t;
- the fifth is the salary he hopes to get for period $(t + 2)$ if he enrolls himself for the second sub-period of t.

The individual then compares the earnings, in present value[2] on the shortest possible significant horizon (two periods), he hopes to get if he searches to the sum of the search cost plus the income without the search cost. Several eventualities are naturally to be examined, but there is no need to go into detail within the framework of this chapter.

---

[2] This supposes the introduction of an individual discount coefficient.

As for the applicant's behaviour, it is obvious for the second sub-period (every job which offers the individual more than the minimum wage is preferable to unemployment), but it is more subtle in the first sub-period since the individual has to determine the level x starting at which he will accept the offers.

That leaves the adaptations of expectations to be considered. This is the object of the following hypotheses:

● There are for every individual upper and lower limits of the value of market observation; that value rises when the individual does not search and reaches its maximum in a finite amount of time; it does not rise when the individual searches.

● If during T consecutive observations, an individual has not found, in the second sub-period, an available job for the following period offering more than y, he does not expect, in the second sub-period of t, to get more than y for the period $(t + 1)$. (Naturally, an analogous hypothesis is made for the remuneration hoped for in period $(t + 2)$.)

Under the preceding hypotheses, the market converges in probability to a stable state, but there obviously exist numerous stable states in addition to traditional equilibrium. These states are neither efficient nor concentrated.

Interpretation of the results

In this model, the individuals may be divided into two categories:

● the passive individuals for whom the maximum value of market observation is inferior to the search cost;
● the active individuals for whom such is not the case.

In a stable state the employed active individuals continue to search from time to time in order to see whether they can find better remuneration on the market. The more active they are, the more frequent this search. These are the individuals who set off new market dynamics if the supply and demand curves are modified.

As for the passive individuals, after having searched in a transient manner in the course of the process, they stop searching definitively from a certain date on, as the estimation they make of their hopes for supplementary earnings does not compensate, as they see it, the loss resulting from the search.

The situation of these two categories of individuals in a stable state is highly different:

- active employed individuals are paid a maximum wage observed on the market; this wage is at least equal to the equilibrium price p but may be substantially higher;
- employed passive individuals may receive any one of the wages paid on the market;
- employed active individuals hold jobs among the first K jobs (that is, those which would be filled in the traditional equilibrium);
- employed passive individuals may hold jobs which would remain vacant in the traditional equilibrium (that is, the 'inefficient' jobs);
- naturally if the first K individuals are active, the only stable states correspond to traditional equlibrium.

It can be shown that the higher the number of active individuals, the lower the maximum wage observed. On the other hand, this wage rises when the number of inefficient jobs held increases.

In other words, the efficient active individuals may benefit from the presence of passive individuals, but, on the other hand, the latter may block the efficient jobs (that is with a high $\bar{v}_i$) at mediocre wage levels.

This model is interesting for more reasons than one:

- The individuals are not like molecules, limited by the actions of preceding models. They use their past observations to build expectations and to adapt them.
- The driving force comes from active individuals who deem it advisable to observe the market from time to time in order to assure themselves that no improvement of their situation can be made. These individuals take advantage of their search efforts by obtaining the best wages on the market.
- The appearance of new stable states stems from the existence of passive individuals among the individuals who should normally be employed.

Here we can see to what extent those who proclaim the efficiency of the market under all circumstances are mistaken since this efficiency depends fundamentally—among other things—on the psychological attitude of the agents. A market with few active agents will carry out only a partial sorting of individuals and jobs and maintain a noticeable wage dispersion.

In human society, initiative, the will to explore, and the constant questioning of what exists may be more or less rewarding behaviour and consequently more or less frequent. As a result, depending on the social environment, the markets may prove to be more or less efficient institutions for the allocation of economic resources.

The upsetting role of passiveness on the part of economic agents may have more far-reaching consequences than simple market disorganization. There is nothing easier than to imagine a few examples:

- by reducing the surplus (without information costs) in a stable state, it may make investment impossible as a result of the decrease in savings and the amount of taxes paid;
- by increasing the maximum wage paid on the market, it makes launching new ventures more difficult since these activities draw first of all active individuals, who will be demanding in matters of remuneration;
- by allowing efficient positions to remain vacant, it hinders the development of activities generative of future surpluses.

The activity and passivity of individuals affect not only the total surplus. They also influence its distribution. Certain firms have to concede salaries above an equilibrium price. Others manage to keep passive manual labour on at low salaries. The market ends up by exploding into a multitude of local situations with exploitation[3] of one agent by another. Sometimes it is the active individual who, through potential mobility, obtains a better salary from the firm. Sometimes it is the firm which takes advantage of its employees' reluctance to search. But not all passive individuals are exploited. They may have the chance of being correctly paid. The stable state in which the market ends up is in fact undetermined. It is the result of the uncertainties of history.

The introduction of irreversibilities has therefore put us in the presence of dynamics very different from the 'reversible' dynamics of the preceding chapter. From now on, the future is no longer plotted out. A whole array of stable states can coexist and constitute for other markets the points of departure of different future trajectories.[4] History and its uncertainties may lead the market to a promising

---

[3] In comparison to the surplus sharing of traditional equilibrium.
[4] If the evolution of other markets is conditioned by the volumes and price levels occurring on this market.

stable state or trap it in states implying the definitive abandonment of certain hopes.

We are, however, still at the point of analysing these elementary aspects of organization.

4

The Market and Increasing Yields

Observation of industrial economies brings forth the frequent existence of increasing yields: whether it concerns the effects connected with research, the size of equipment, or the cumulative production already attained. Hence the interest in exploring the operation of the simple model in Chapter 2 when firms, instead of offering a single job, offer several, the new receipts of the marginal job increasing or decreasing in relation to the number of jobs already taken. This interest can be justified by analysis, which will confirm the economist's intuition and show that, under certain conditions, the presence of increasing yields may make the market converge towards inefficient stable states.

The study of the dynamics of the labour-market in the presence of increasing yields shows that its evolution depends on the crossing of two hypotheses, one concerning the jumps of scale, the other the circulation of information.

So, before proposing a model and presenting its results, it is appropriate to think about the formulation of these two sets of hypotheses.

The Hypotheses

As stated above, we shall introduce in turn the hypotheses concerning jumps of scale, following them with those explaining the conditions for the circulation of information.

Jumps of scale

The simplest model consists of assuming that each firm i disposes of two jobs, the total net receipts being equal to $\bar{v}^1$ if only one position is filled and to $\bar{v}^1 + \bar{v}^2$ if both positions are filled.[1] The firm has an increasing yield if $\bar{v}^2 > \bar{v}^1$ and a decreasing (or constant) yield if $\bar{v}^2 > \bar{v}^1$ (or $\bar{v}^2 = \bar{v}^1$).

When the firm has a decreasing yield, it is always in its interest to start filling the first position, and it takes interest in the second only if the first is filled. It matters little, therefore, whether it knows $\bar{v}^2$ at the start or whether this value is only revealed once it has experience at the first level of production, because the development of the company is carried out (though it may be over a short period of time) by increasing its size progressively.

The situation is entirely different when the firm has an increasing yield. Indeed, production on a second level can then be profitable while production on the first level is not. For this reason a firm may be faced with several different situations:

- it knows from the start $\bar{v}^1$ and $\bar{v}^2$ and is technically capable of operating at level 2 right away;
- it initially knows only $\bar{v}^1$, and $\bar{v}^2$ is revealed only if it is already operating at level 1; in other words, experience of the first level is necessary in order to be capable of benefiting from the economies of scale at the second;
- it initially knows only $\bar{v}^1$ but anticipates the existence of increasing yield and takes the risk, under certain conditions, of operating right away at level 2;
- it initially knows only $\bar{v}^1$ but can obtain $\bar{v}^2$ in exchange for a cost of information (or transfer of technology) c_i.

These four situations illustrate real industrial configurations: the first corresponds to a firm which perfectly masters its production techniques and is consequently capable of making jumps in scale without significant risk; the second describes, on the contrary, a company which cannot afford to skip the learning experience of size; the third illustrates the case of an innovative firm which attempts immediate large-scale exploitation of a new technique; the fourth accents the possibility of a firm's acquiring the technology which will permit it to take a short cut past intermediary scales.

Of these four cases, only the first two—for the sake of brevity—will be treated in this chapter.

---

[1] Naturally, net receipts depend on the firm. The index i is omitted to simplify notation when there is no risk of ambiguity.

The circulation of information

In order to decide whether to be present on the work market, individuals need previous information concerning wages, but the information they are likely to obtain may differ in nature, depending upon whether it concerns wages at a constant or variable level of firm activity:

- a first possibility is that firms having a certain level of activity announce to the workers the wages offered for that level of activity;
- a second eventuality is that firms let the workers know the wages they intend to pay if they are capable of operating at the different levels of production conceived.

As the wages at a constant level of activity are in effect the only ones in operation, for simplicity's sake we shall name these two hypotheses actual salaries and salaries planned. The crossing of these alternatives can be seen in the four cases shown in Table 4.1.

TABLE 4.1

| | Announcement of salaries | |
	Actual	Planned
No jumps of scale	1	3
Existence of jumps of scale	2	4

As we shall see, the stable states in which the market will end up differ noticeably in the four cases shown.

The Model

This will be described as for case 1, in which every firm is able to recruit two workers immediately, but announces, if it has an activity, only the wages offered for that level of activity.

There are present on the labour-market m individuals ($l \le k \le m$), each individual having a reservation wage $\underline{w}_k$, such that he will not agree to work for lower wages.

Each period is broken down into two successive sub-periods:

- a search sub-period during which contacts between individuals and firms take place, followed by transactions between the agents who made contact, these transactions serving to define the work contracts for the second sub-period;
- a work sub-period during which the preceding contracts are carried out.

During this work sub-period, company i pays salary $s(i)$ and, depending on the number of persons it employs (0, 1, or 2 persons), makes a profit of 0, $[\bar{v}^1 - s(i)]$, or $[\bar{v}^1 + \bar{v}^2 - 2s(i)]$. The values $\bar{v}_i^1$, $\bar{v}_i^2$ $\underline{w}_k$, $s(i)$ are assumed to be integers.

These preliminary elements permit the successive introduction of the notion of a state of the market, the situation before the contacts, and the contacts.

The notion of a state of the market

By definition a state e_t of the market during a period t is characterized by a set of five applications:

- the first defines the distribution of the individuals among the firms during the work sub-period, some individuals possibly being unemployed;
- the second defines the salaries paid at the end of the work sub-period;
- the third characterizes the salaries demanded by the individuals during the search sub-period;
- finally the last two define the salaries the companies plan on during the search sub-period: more precisely, company i plans on paying salary $v^1(i)$ if it employs one worker and salary $v^2(i)$ if it employs two workers.

The situation before the contacts

Individuals are naturally going to try to improve their salary. It may therefore be assumed that for period t they will ask for one unit more than they had for the preceding period. In the same way, the companies will try to increase their benefits by setting the salaries planned in such a manner that:

- if they had a profit in period $(t - 1)$, they will increase that profit by 1 and eventually by 2 units at least;[2]
- if they took a loss during period $(t - 1)$, they will make a profit of 1 or eventually 2.

But companies having to pay all their personnel the same salary must choose which among the contemplated salaries to announce. We shall suppose that they assume the recruitment of one worker if they employed 0 or 1 worker in the preceding period and the recruitment of two workers if they employed two, and that it is on this basis that the individuals will be able to gather information on the general state of the salaries proposed.

The salaries $a_t(i)$ announced by the companies are therefore such that:

$$\begin{cases} a_t(i) = v^1(i) \text{ if } i \text{ employs 0 or 1 worker in } (t - 1) \\ a_t(i) = v^2(i) \text{ if } i \text{ employs 2 workers in } (t - 1) \end{cases} \tag{1}$$

Relationship (1) expresses the hypothesis of the announcement of the actual salary. It corresponds, as can be seen, to the communication:

- of salaries offered for ongoing activity by active firms suffering no losses;
- of salaries planned for the first level of production by inactive firms or those recording a loss.[3]

At the beginning of period t, each individual k gathers information on the general state of the salaries announced on the market so that he can decide whether or not he will search for a job. To do so, he draws on a random sub-set of firms such that each firm may have a non-zero probability of being drawn and sees the salaries announced by the firms in that sample. He decides to become active on the labour-market if at least two announcements are above his asking salary.[4]

---

[2] The fact that the companies witness, according to the case, a rise in profits of one or two units stems from having stipulated that the salaries be whole numbers.

[3] The precise formulation is a bit more complex than announced at the start of the chapter, as firms not in a situation of normal activity must be taken into account.

[4] The fact that an individual becomes active only if two announcements are above the salary he is asking is necessary for convergence of the state of the market towards a stable state. The constraint results from the fact that each enterprise can recruit 0, 1, or 2 workers.

At this point, the information received by the individuals differs from one individual to another. It is moreover anonymous, since it is assumed that the individuals are only interested in the general salary level and for the time being do not care which companies propose the determined salaries.

The contacts

After the preceding phase during which the workers have individually decided whether to be present on the market — that is, available or not for a new job — the companies begin a search for actual applicants. To do so they become successively active on the market in random order.

When company i enters the market, it draws on a random subgroup of workers, such that every worker has a non-zero probability of being drawn on. It then offers a salary $\sigma_t(i)$ such that:

$$\begin{cases} \sigma_t(i) = v_t^1(i) \text{ if card } M_t^i \leq 1 \\ \sigma_t(i) = \sup\{v_t^1(i), v_t^2(i)\} \text{ if card } M_t^i \geq 2 \end{cases} \tag{2}$$

M_t^i designating the set of active individuals discovered by company i having as yet not signed a work contract for period t.

Relationship (2) expresses the hypothesis of the absence of jumps of scale effects.

As for the individuals in M_t^i they break down into two categories:

- inside individuals employed by the company during period $(t - 1)$ and not having signed with another company as yet for period t;
- the interested outside applicants.

It is then possible to describe the company in all the situations it runs into and which are defined by:

- the number of inside individuals (0, 1, or 2);
- the number of outside applicants (0, 1, 2 or more);
- the level of the salaries offered.

Therefore, to give an example, if there are at least one inside individual and two outside applicants the company may find itself in the following situations:

- $\sigma_t(i) = v_t^1(i)$: it fires the inside individual and recruits an individual drawn uniformly at random from among the outside applicants;
- $\sigma_t(i) = v_t^2(i)$ and, taking (2) into account: $v_t^2(i) > v_t^1(i)$: the company fires the inside individual if he refuses its proposition and recruits two individuals drawn uniformly at random from among the outside applicants; the company keeps the inside individual on if he accepts its proposition and recruits an individual drawn uniformly at random from among the outside applicants.

The hypotheses which have just been outlined define a homogeneous Markovian stochastic process of market change. Moreover, the salaries being bounded and the model discrete, there is but a finite number of states possible.

The other variants of the model

These assume the modification of at least one hypothesis concerning jumps of scale or the circulation of information.

Jumps of scale If, for technical (and human) reasons, a company cannot go directly from level 0 to level 2, relationship (2) must be replaced by the relationship:

$$\begin{cases} \sigma_t(i) = v_t^1(i) \text{ if card } M_t^i \leq 1 \text{ or if } i \in N_{t-1}^0 \\ \sigma_t(i) = \sup \{v_t^2(i)\} \text{ if card } M_t^i \geq 2 \text{ and if } i \notin N_{t-1}^0 \end{cases} \quad (2b)$$

N_{t-1}^0 designating the set of companies employing no worker in period $(t-1)$.

Circulation of information The alternative hypothesis, which has been called the 'announcement of planned salaries', is that the companies communicate their salary intentions at diverse levels of production. The announcement made by a company i is then made up of the pair $\{v_t^1(i), v_t^2(i)\}$.

In fact, it may be shown that it amounts to replacing relationship (1) by the relationship:

$$a_t(i) = \sup \{v_t^1(i), v_t^2(i)\} \quad (1b)$$

It might seem that, with the announcement of the wages planned (at varying levels of activity), individuals would be better informed. In fact, this is not necessarily so, because the salary announced by a firm which believes it to be possible may not be so in reality. It is, rather, the content of information which changes from one hypothesis to another, since it concerns, in one case, wages very close to those in operation and, in another case, wages which can only be envisaged.

TABLE 4.2

	Announcement of salaries	
	Actual	Planned
No jumps of scale	1. (1) (2)	3. (1*b*) (2)
Existence of jumps of scale	2. (1) (2*b*)	4. (1*b*) (2*b*)

Table 4.2 is a review of the relations which define the four variants, from which it is now possible to present the results.

Results

These can be examined from the angle of convergence of the market towards a stable state, the characteristics of stable states, and the efficiency properties of these states in the four variants of the model.

Convergence towards a stable state

With the following hypotheses:

- for the highest wage planned there is an excess of labour demand and for the lowest wage planned an excess of supply;
- each of the parameters $\underline{w}_k$, $\bar{v}_i^1$, $\bar{v}_i^2$, $[\bar{v}_i^1 + \bar{v}_i^2]/2$ is distinct from the others;
- the information is as extensive for the wages announced as for the firms' offers

it can be shown that stable states exist in all the variants of the model and that the market converges towards a stable state in finite time with a probability of 1 whatever the variant considered.

Characteristics of the stable states

Let E_1, E_2, E_3, and E_4 be the set of stable states in variants 1 to 4.

The offers being higher in variants 3 and 4, any individual likely to be an applicant in variants 1 and 2 is all the more likely to be so in variants 3 and 4. Consequently: $E_3 \subset E_1$ and $E_4 \subset E_2$.

In the same manner, introducing jumps of scale restricts the set of possible successors to a state, and therefore can only increase the set of stable states which implies $E_1 \subset E_2$ and $E_3 \subset E_4$.

Lastly, it is possible to show that every stable state of variant 2 is a stable state of variant 1; which gives us $E_1 = E_2$. Indeed, effects of scale only affect inactive firms which in variants 1 and 2 offer a wage rate planned for production level 1. In a stable state of variant 2, the offer is sufficient to keep these firms from trying to produce at level 2 and ensures a stable state in variant 1.

On the other hand, counter-examples show that E_2 is not always equal to E_4 nor E_3 to E_4.

The sets of stable states therefore verify the relations:

$$E_3 \subset E_4 \subset E_2 \qquad E_2 = E_1 \tag{3}$$

Thus, the conjunction of the announcement of planned salaries and the absence of jumps of scale reduces the number of stable states to a minimum, while at the other extreme the announcement of actual salaries increases the number of these states to a maximum.

Moreover, whatever the set of hypotheses, the stable states have the following two properties:

- in a stable state, there is at most one individual ready to change jobs;
- in a stable state, the actual wage rate on the market is 'nearly unique', this expression meaning that the single wage is realized to within a unit (this results from the discrete nature of the model) and to within two firms at the most (this results from the type of job application chosen); the two exceptions cannot both be superior or inferior to the price given by the other firms.

Efficiency properties of stable states

A few preliminary definitions are indispensable before introducing these properties.

1. We shall call market structure the pair made up of:

- the partition of set M of individuals into sub-sets M^0 of unemployed individuals and M^1 of employed individuals;
- the partition of set N of firms into three sub-sets N^0 of inactive firms, N^1 of firms in operation with one position, N^2 of firms in operation with two positions.

These definitions imply that:

$$\text{Card } M^1 = \text{card } N^1 + 2 \text{ card } N^2 \qquad (4)$$

Clearly, two stable states corresponding to the same market structure differ only in the distribution of the individuals among the various jobs and are therefore indistinguishable in the sense given to this term in Chapter 2.

2. Two market structures (M^1, N^1, N^2) and $M'^1, N'^1, N'^2)$ will be called adjacent if:[5]

$$\begin{cases} \text{card } [M^1 \, \Delta \, M'^1] \le 1 \; \text{card } [N^1 \, \Delta \, N'^1] \le 2 \\ \text{card } [N^2 \, \Delta \, N'^2] \le 2 \end{cases} \qquad (5)$$

In ordinary language, these relations mean that the market structures are very close. Therefore two states whose structures are adjacent will be qualified as nearly indistinguishable.

3. With a market structure will be associated a surplus:

$$S = \sum_{i \in N^1} \bar{v}1 + \sum_{i \in N^2} (\bar{v}^1 + \bar{v}^2) - \sum_{k \in M^1} w_k \qquad (6)$$

4. Lastly, a market structure will be said to be efficient if it maximizes the surplus on all market structures.

With the help of these definitions, it is possible to demonstrate that the states in E_3 are nearly indistinguishable and their market structures are adjacent to the efficient structure. In other words, the absence of jumps of scale and the announcement of planned wage rates ensures efficient operation of the market even in the presence of increasing yields.

---

[5] The symbol Δ designates, as usual, symmetric difference.

On the other hand, the situation is not the same in the three other cases: the set of stable states then contains states whose structures are not adjacent to the structure of the efficient market.

Thus, in keeping with the intuition of every professional economist, the existence of jumps of scale or the announcement of actual wages may, in the presence of increasing yields, block the market in stable states far from efficient market structures.

At this point, the probable link between jumps of scale and the circulation of information must be emphasized. When there are jumps of scale, a business firm i which is not in activity has poor knowledge of $\bar{v}_i^2$ and therefore can hardly announce $v_i^2(i)$. The message that it then sends probably concerns the actual wages jumps and not the possible wages. It is normal, on the other hand, that in the absence of jumps of scale, firm i should communicate the possible wages since the absence of constraint on its level of activity means that it disposes of sound information on its operation at every level imaginable. Consequently, the two most realistic cases are 2 and 3.

Thus the difficulty a firm has in operating at a given level of capacity without learning about operation at a lower capacity might trap the market in stable states far removed from efficient states. Phenomena of this sort take place frequently in contemporary economies:

- certain industrial activities may not spring up in developing countries since it is impossible to start them up at a level which would make them profitable;
- within the countries of the USA-Japan-Western Europe Triad, an industrial group can often only remain on the market if the share it holds or the cumulated production it has achieved allow it to reduce its costs to a competitive level.

A number of potentially efficient activities are thus blocked in their development by market dynamics when increasing yield exists. Naturally, nothing permits us to assert a priori that the firms so trapped by the market would be more efficient at higher levels of capacity than the firms already operating at these levels. There are, however, two types of firm behaviour which may contribute to getting the market out of the inefficient stable states in which it may be confined:

- the purchase of technology, a firm having hopes of operating straightaway at a high level in exchange for information costs;[6]
- acceptance of the risks of scale, a firm anticipating the existence of increasing yield and accepting the gamble of immediately setting up a high capacity without precise knowledge of the resulting costs.[7]

Brief as they may be, these few considerations show that the study of self-organization phenomena are not only of theoretical interest; they also permit a fuller understanding of today's realities.

---

[6] Experience has nevertheless shown the difficulty of technology transfers when the purchasing firm does not already have experience in large-scale industrial activities.

[7] Such gambles are frequently accepted by large industrial groups in developed countries, notably Japan.

5

The Traditional Market

The time has now come to take a look at a more complex market in which a connection will be made between two categories of agent interested in the same unstockable goods:

- individual buyers, the purchasing intentions of individual k taking the form of a demand, which is a decreasing function of the price and nul for any price above or equal to a price limit particular to each individual;
- retailers choosing at the start of each period the quantity of goods that they will buy in view of sales and the firm sales price they will propose throughout the entire period.

The additional complexity has a double origin: on the one hand each individual may buy a greater or lesser quantity of goods and on the other each retailer has to make two decisions, one concerning the quantity placed at the buyers' disposal, the other about the price proposed.

Four situations will be studied:

- in the first, the buyers will see at random at least two sellers each period, every seller being likely to be seen each period by each buyer; in addition all the sellers will have identical characteristics and will bear, in particular, the same unit 'production' cost for acquiring and presenting the unit of goods to be sold;
- in the second situation, the sellers will still have identical characteristics, but in each period, every buyer will simply go to see his usual seller and will only search for other offers if the price this seller gives him is above an acceptable limit that he has set himself beforehand;
- the third situation is a mixture of the first two, part of the buyers behaving as in the first situation and part of them as in the second;
- the last situation then assumes that the various retailers have

different production costs; the same hypotheses as in the first situation hold as to the individuals.

One paragraph will be devoted to each of the last three situations and two to the first, the presentation of the results being followed in this case by an example aimed at providing fuller understanding of agents' behaviour and market dynamics. For the sake of convenience, I shall describe the buyers as 'mobile' in the first situation and 'conservative' in the second.

Identical Retailers and Mobile Buyers

In keeping with our usual order of presentation, we will now study buyers' behaviour, retailers' behaviour, the existence of stable states, and convergence towards those states.

Buyers' behaviour

Each buyer k is endowed with a non-increasing demand function in whole values $f_k(p)$ such that $f_k(p) = 0$ for $p \geq \bar{p}_k$, $\bar{p}_k$ being individual k's characteristic price ceiling.

During each period, all the buyers become active on the market once and only once, one after the other, and in random order. When his turn comes, a buyer draws a random sample of retailers (every retailer having a non-zero probability of being drawn). He adds to this sample his privileged retailer from the preceding period—if there is one—and collects information on the prices offered by the sellers in this enlarged sample.

The privileged retailer in any period is the supplier in the enlarged sample who offers the lowest price on the condition that this price be inferior to $\bar{p}_k$. If there are several retailers in this situation, the retailer chosen is the privileged retailer of the previous period if he figures among them, or, if such is not the case, he is drawn at random from within the group. Of course, there may be no privileged retailer.

The buyer's adding of his privileged retailer's offer to the other offers discovered during the period is a way of taking into account the information transmitted. As in the model with information search costs, this hypothesis is necessary to the convergence of the market towards a stable state.

As for the individuals' buying procedure, it may be characterized in a natural manner by the following: buyer k chooses out of the enlarged sample the buyer or one of the buyers offering the lowest price and—on the condition that this price be inferior to $\bar{p}_k$—tries to obtain the desired quantity from him. If the total demand cannot be satisfied (for lack of stock), the buyer tries to obtain the remainder from other retailers of the enlarged sample, consulting them in order of increasing price. He ceases to be active on the market when his demand is met or when the retailers of the enlarged sample have nothing left to sell at an acceptable price. With each procedure, the buyer re-evaluates his demand level on the basis of the average price that he would pay if the remainder of his demand were met at this stage.

Retailers' behaviour

At the beginning of each period t, the retailers must choose the quantity and the price offered, in view of past observations and knowing that the goods cannot be stocked for the next period.

We shall moreover say that every retailer can procure any quantity whatever of goods at constant and whole unit price c, this price being the same for all the retailers.

But how can retailers' behaviour be described when it takes into account as little information as possible while remaining reasonably rational and sufficiently general?

It is first of all normal to assume that with every price $p(t)$ for period t, a retailer can associate a quantity $q(t)$, the pair $\{p(t), q(t)\}$ constituting a retailer policy.

We shall then say that a retailer has some recall of policies adopted in the past and the demand and profit that these policies created, but we shall limit this recall to one period. In other words at the end of period t, a retailer knows the profit, the price offered, the quantity put up for sale, and the demand received for period $(t-1)$ and t.

How will he go about choosing $p(t+1)$ and $q(t+1)$? One thing is certain: he will try in period $(t+1)$ not only to make a positive profit but to make a higher profit than in period t. He can nevertheless not be sure of getting such results since the demand he will receive in period $(t+1)$ is a random variable.

These first considerations suggest the introduction of the following two definitions in which the adverb 'potentially' is there to remind us that a quantity q put up for sale may not be totally sold; $\Pi(t)$ designates the profit of period t:

(i) The retailer policy (p, q) is potentially profitable for period $(t + 1)$ if and only if $q > 0$, $p > c$ and $q(p - c) > \Pi(t)$.

(ii) The retailer policy (p, q) is potentially strictly profitable for period $(t + 1)$ if and only if $q > 0$, $p > c$ and:

$$q(p - c) > \Pi(t) \text{ if } \Pi(t) \geq \Pi(t - 1)$$
$$q(p - c) \geq \Pi(t - 1) \text{ if } \Pi(t) < \Pi(t - 1)$$

The second definition implies that when a retailer is faced with a drop in profits, he will try to get back to the profit level of the preceding period.

Starting with these elements we must study the way the retailer chooses prices, quantities, and policies.

The choice of price. Since the retailer has little information at his disposal, it seems normal to assume that he will explore other price levels with caution and avoid large price variations from one period to the next. We shall thus let it be said that, from period t to period $(t + 1)$, he modifies the price by one unit at the most, consequently imagining for $(t + 1)$ the triple $(p, p - 1, p + 1)$. With two restrictions, however, to eliminate unlikely behaviour:

- when the retailer notices that a price change has caused a drop in profits, he will not go any further in that direction;
- if, on the contrary, profits have increased he will consider the difference between his offer and the demand received: an offer below demand leads him to maintain or increase his price, an offer in excess to lower his price, and an offer equal to demand to retain all three options.

The choice of quantities. The retailer associates with price $p, p - 1$, $p + 1$, the quantities $q^p(t + 1)$, $q^{p-1}(t + 1)$ and $q^{p+1}(t + 1)$ in keeping with the following rules of conduct:

1. The retailer believes the demand–price relationship to be negative: he therefore puts up for sale a quantity:

- inferior or equal to the demand received if he increases the price proposed;

- superior or equal to the last demand received if he lowers the price proposed;
- equal to the last demand received if he does not modify his price.

2. The retailer's behaviour is stable: if, from $(t - 1)$ to t, price and demand have not varied, he does not change the quantities associated with the different prices.

3. The retailer reacts to a drop in profits—that is, he 'turns back' if he observes that a change in price has caused a drop in profits; more explicitly if $\Pi(t) < \Pi(t - 1)$, he chooses $q^{p+1}(t + 1)$ and $q^{p-1}(t + 1)$ so that:

- the policy $(p + 1)$ be potentially strictly profitable if the last policy was a price decrease,
- the policy $(p + 1)$ be potentially strictly profitable if the last policy was a price increase.

The choice of policies. Any potentially profitable policy satisfying the above conditions (it can be demonstrated that there always exists at least one) shall be considered acceptable, and it shall be assumed that at each period the retailer chooses at random one of the acceptable policies from among the strictly profitable ones or, in their absence, those which are merely potentially profitable.

Stable states and the problem of convergence

In such a model, a stable state is defined by two conditions:

- no retailer believes it possible to increase profits;
- no buyer has hopes of finding a retailer offering a better price than his privileged retailer (if the latter exists).

It is easy to prove that this definition implies two consequences:

- in a stable state, all the retailers propose the same price;
- in a stable state where the price is superior to $(c+1)$, all the retailers sell a positive quantity.

But, with the hypotheses which have been formed, does the market necessarily converge towards a stable state? The answer to this question is no, since analysis shows that the retailers' short memory and the small amount of information that they use allow indefinite price fluctuations.

All it takes, however—and this result is instructive—is one retailer who adopts a more elaborate behaviour for the market dynamics to be fundamentally modified. It has in fact been shown that, if there is at least one retailer behaving cautiously, the market converges in probability towards a stable state in finite time; in that stable state, the price lies within the interval, bounds included, defined by the minimum $(c + 1)$ and by a maximum such that every retailer has at least one client.

What is a retailer with cautious behaviour? A retailer, who, having at some time in the past, modified his price in a particular way and observed a decrease in the profits he would have made had he been able to meet fully the demand, will never again follow the same price policy.

The definition is unwieldy but its meaning is clear: a cautious retailer will not renew any attempts which, as he sees it, ended in failure.

The presence of such a retailer is enough to stabilize the market, but the price level reached depends on the initial situation and on the history. In other words, if retailers' behaviour is as described up to this point (with at least one cautious retailer), the market converges towards a stable state with a single price, but that price may be superior to $(c + 1)$—and consequently leave the retailers with a rent.

Most of these stable states, however, are not robust (like the pseudo-equilibria of solutions in suspension) since it only takes one more hypothesis, the existence of a retailer with competitive behaviour, to draw the market convergence towards a stable state with a minimum price $(c + 1)$.

A retailer with competitive behaviour is one who considers that a price decrease proportionally creates a demand increase superior in absolute value to the decrease that would be brought on by a price rise.

Three aspects of this analysis are worthy of attention:

1. First of all, in a situation where the retailers are incapable of observing price distribution on the market, the fact that at each stage they explore neighbouring price policies, attempt to improve profits, and will not persist with policies which have proved to be inefficient are not enough to ensure the convergence of the market towards a stable state.

2. Nevertheless, that convergence is certain, a single price will be established on the market, if one of the retailers shows cautious behaviour—that is, he does not believe it possible to improve his profits (in the precise sense mentioned above) by following a policy which was not favourable the last time it was chosen. However, the presence of such a retailer is not enough to lower the market price to its minimum. In other words, the set of stable states may be divided into sub-sets corresponding to the different market prices possible, the stable states differing within each sub-set in the distribution of sales among retailers and the allocation of buyers to retailers.

3. For the price to be at a minimum, the existence of a second retailer, distinct from the first, is a necessity. This retailer must exhibit competitive behaviour—that is, believe that whatever his past experience he will draw numerous buyers by lowering his price.

One last remark: since no capacity constraint has been introduced as concerns the retailers, the stable states at a minimum price may be such that only one retailer may actually sell on the market. The persistence of these states stems from the fact that the model assumes the other retailers to be potentially active and ready to intervene if the price goes up. An example will help to illustrate the points made in this paragraph.

An example of market dynamics

Let there be a very simple market with two retailers and two buyers. The supply cost is equal to 5 and the buyers have the same demand function:

$$f(p) = 2 \text{ if } p \leq 6$$
$$f(p) = 1 \text{ if } p = 7 \text{ or } 8$$
$$f(p) = 0 \text{ if } p \geq 9$$

Initially, the first retailer offers $q_1 = 1$ and proposes the price $p_1 = 7$ while the second offers $q_2 = 1$ and proposes the price $p_2 = 11$. Since it has been accepted that every buyer sees at least two sellers, the two retailers will always be seen by both buyers.

Let us assume that the first retailer is cautious. We shall show: (i) that the market can be blocked in a stable state at a price superior to $(c + 1)$, (ii) why the market necessarily converges towards a stable state at a single price, (iii) why the competitive behaviour exhibited by the second retailer reduces the price to $(c + 1)$.

(i) during period 0, the demands received by retailers 1 and 2 amount to 2 and 0 respectively.

Period 1. The first retailer, having observed a demand excess, decides to increase his price, while the second lowers his, seeing that he believes the demand–price relationship to be negative. Therefore:

$$p_1 = 8, q_1 = 1 \qquad p_2 = 10, q_2 = 1$$

Consequently $d_1 = 2$ and $d_2 = 0$

Period 2. The retailers continue to modify their respective prices in the same direction. Therefore:

$$p_1 = 9, q_1 = 1 \qquad p_2 = 9, q_2 = 1$$

The buyers find the prices too high and stop their purchases:

$$d_1 = 0 \qquad d_2 = 0$$

while the first retailer who is cautious decides never to increase his price again from 8 to 9.

Period 3. The two retailers lower their prices:

$$p_1 = 8, q_1 = 1 \qquad p_2 = 8, q_2 = 1$$

Each retailer supplies a buyer. Offers and demands adjust to each other.

Period 4. The two retailers who, in the preceding period, recorded an increase in profits continue in the same direction:

$$p = 7, q_1 = 2 \qquad p_2 = 7, q_2 = 2$$

(they must in fact increase their offer in order for the price decrease to be potentially strictly profitable). Each retailer keeps his buyer but observes an offer in excess.

Period 5. The two retailers increase their prices:

$$p_1 = 8, q_1 = 1 \qquad p_2 = 8, q_2 = 1$$

The first retailer who is cautious will no longer modify his price. As a result, if the expectations of the second are such that he does not wish to change prices, the market will be locked in a stable state at price $p = 8$, each retailer having one client.

(ii) Let us now show why a stable state is necessarily attained. Retailer 1 being cautious cannot indefinitely fluctuate his price among the three values 6, 7, and 8 since, notably due to the finite number of buyers, such a policy cannot lead to an indefinite rise in profits. Therefore, after a certain amount of time, he fixes the price at one of these values.

(*a*) The first retailer fixes his price at 8: if the second retailer is at the same price and does not wish to modify his price, the market is in the stable state described earlier. If the second retailer proposes $p_2 = 9$, he observes $d_2 = 0$ and must reduce his price to 7 in two stages. The consequence: $p_2 = 7$, $q_2 = 2$, he attracts the entire demand. Observing a demand at zero, the first retailer is obliged to reduce his price to 7 and since he is cautious he will never raise it again. The only prices possible for him then are 6 and 7, which correspond to cases (*b*) and (*c*).

(*b*) The first retailer fixes his price at 7: the analysis is identical; a stable state can be attained at $p = 7$ with one client per retailer or the first retailer must propose a price of 6 (case (*c*)).

(*c*) The first retailer fixes his price at 6: if the second retailer does not wish to modify his price when it is itself equal to 6 (which is necessary for the second retailer to sell), a stable state is reached, each of the retailers having one client or one of the retailers supplying the entire demand; if, on the contrary, the second retailer again proposes a price of 7, both buyers choose the first retailer who will indefinitely supply the entire demand.

This example shows how the market can be trapped at a price higher than $(c + 1)$. Several factors contribute to making this eventuality come about: sellers' expectations, the price policies sellers choose, the buyers' level of information. In the above example, it is the fact that, after a while, the retailers modify their prices simultaneously and in the same direction and consequently do not lose their buyers which makes the existence of a stable state at $p = 8$ possible. The buyers' level of information may have important consequences if the retailers are more numerous. Indeed, in such a case, the market may be trapped without simultaneous price changes if the buyers are unable to find the least expensive retailers in time.

(iii) If the second retailer behaves competitively, he will not maintain his price at level 8 in case (*a*) nor at 7 in case (*b*). Consequently, a stable state is possible only at $p = 6$.

It seemed useful to develop this example a little in order to show:

- that with retailers behaving reasonably a number of roads are possible and lead to a number of stable states;
- that the existence of one retailer behaving competitively is enough to reduce the price to its minimum.

What will become of these results when certain hypotheses of the model are changed? This will be the subject-matter of the next three paragraphs.

Identical Retailers and Conservative Buyers

Several authors (Diamond 1971, Hey 1974, Axell 1977, Salop and Stiglitz 1977) have stressed that the presence, implicit or explicit, of positive information costs for all buyers might imply the existence of an equilibrium at a monopolistic price.

With the exception of Hey, all these authors postulate that the buyers' information search is sequential or that the buyers have a fixed reserve price and only see one retailer chosen at random during a period. The underlying reasoning is then that presented by Stiglitz (1979): if all the buyers have identical information costs, a retailer can, in the course of a period, raise his price by an amount inferior to the information costs without losing a client. Thus, in time, all the retailers will arrive at a monopolistic price. Such reasoning may nevertheless be contested when information costs are explicit, since it does not take into account the buyers, possibility of evaluating what they may possibly have to gain in the future from the search for information before deciding whether or not to seek information.[1] As a matter of fact, the reasoning is no longer valid if the buyers anticipate the sellers' strategy.

As for Hey, he assumes that in every period the buyers systematically see a sample of sellers, but he introduces a particular price distribution which implies that each retailer keeps his rank in that distribution. He introduces, as well, an infinite number of buyers which results in a retailer always having clients.

[1] This phenomenon was examined in Ch. 3.

Hence the interest in modifying the initial model in order to bring out the set of hypotheses ensuring convergence of the market in probability towards a stable state at a monopolistic price.

Three modifications will be made:

1. The buyers will all have the same demand function $f(p)$ and the profits generated by a buyer $f(p)(p - c)$ will be a concave function reaching its maximum in p^* ($p^* < \bar{p}_k$ for every k).

2. A buyer k who, at the end of period $(t - 1)$ has a privileged retailer, contacts only that retailer in period t, buys from that retailer only if the price proposed is below $\bar{p}_k$, and does not buy in the opposite case. A buyer k who does not have a privileged retailer chooses another retailer at random.

3. As far as retailers are concerned, the existing hypotheses on cautious and competitive retailers will be replaced by the hypothesis that all the retailers will adopt learning behaviour. Learning behaviour is more constrictive for a retailer than cautious behaviour: not only must the retailer not explore a price change which in the past engendered a drop in the maximum possible profit, but he must be convinced that it will be potentially strictly profitable to renew the proposal of a price change which in the past resulted in a rise in the maximum possible profit.

These three modifications ensure that the market will henceforth converge in finite time towards a stable state at monopolistic price p^*. Thus, even in situations which outwardly have every aspect of competition, the price established on the market may be a monopolistic price. All it takes for this to be so, is that buyers be lazy in their search for information and that sellers learn their lesson from past experiences.

Identical Retailers and Heterogeneous Buyers

One reason for the existence in certain models of states of equilibrium with price dispersion is the simultaneous presence of two types of buyer, the first type of buyer comparing prices before buying and the second being content with contacting a retailer (Salop and Stiglitz 1977, Wilde and Schwartz 1979).

The preceding model allows us to explore such situations starting with the following hypotheses:

- buyers' demands are identical and there is a monopolistic price p^*;
- the set of buyers may be divided into two sub-groups, the sub-group M_1 of conservative buyers (m_1 in number) and the subset M_2 of mobile buyers (m_2 in number);
- all the retailers show learning behaviour.

It can be shown that, with these hypotheses, the market converges in probability in finite time towards a stable state at a single price or with price dispersion.

One condition sufficient for there to be a single price is that all the active retailers in the stable state have mobile clients. In other terms, when $m_2/(m_1 + m_2)$ increases, the probability of market convergence towards a single price state increases.

If the stable state is one with price dispersion, the mobile buyers will necessarily be supplied at the lowest price observed. Here we find another aspect of a conclusion already discussed in Chapter 3.

As for the shape of price distribution, it depends on market dynamics. The maximum number of different prices observed is $(n_1 + 1)$, n_1 designating the number of retailers having only conservative buyers in the stable state. In fact, these retailers cannot increase their price to p^* because they may have lost mobile buyers in the past by raising their price.

Different Retailers

One last situation remains to be examined, that in which the various retailers have different production costs (c_j will designate the production costs for retailer j, $1 \leq j \leq n$).

Three market characteristics are interesting to note in this case:

(i) If the buyers are mobile and if the retailer with the lowest production cost adopts a cautious behaviour pattern, the market converges towards a stable state at a single price p. In this state all the retailers whose production cost is such that $c_j + 1 < p$ sell strictly positive quantities. The price is not necessarily the minimum price. For this to be so, it is necessary:

- either for all buyers to contact all sellers at each stage and the market to start off in an initial state in which the prices proposed by the sellers are distinct;

● or for the retailer with the lowest price to have a behaviour pattern which is not only cautious but competitive.

(ii) If the buyers are conservative, if all retailers adopt a learning behaviour pattern, and if certain production costs are above the monopolistic price, the stable state attained by the market may be one with price dispersion.

(iii) On the other hand, if all production costs are below the monopolistic price, the stable state attained by the market, with conservative buyers and retailers having learning behaviour patterns, is a stable state with a single price equal to the monopolistic price.

It is clear that the variety of results obtained—a variety which is confirmed in the literature—is in itself an important discovery. A discovery worthy of reflection.

The Diversity of Market Dynamics

Table 5.1 recapitulates the principal conclusions, two stable states being considered identical when they correspond to the same price distribution. The diversity of dynamics is clear: in relation to the hypotheses on the buyers' search procedures and on the retailers' behaviour and production costs, we can observe the convergence or absence of convergence towards a stable state, the convergence towards the perfect competition price or towards the monopolistic price, and a single equilibrium price or price dispersion.

The influence of buyers' behaviour on the results has already been considered in Chapter 3. What is new here is the decisive role of the retailers. This behaviour is much richer than in the models in foregoing chapters since the retailer must simultaneously determine the price and the quantity and since he is faced with the very difficult problem of trying to increase his revenue while disposing of very little information. From here on, the retailers' personal characteristics will condition the nature of change in the market, contrary to what is usually taught in micro-economic theory. If the retailers have little memory, the market may fluctuate indefinitely with no stable price imposing itself upon the agents. A cautious retailer entering the scene (being supplied at the lowest cost) allows the appearance of a price. The adopting of learning behaviour by all allows them to draw—if the buyers

TABLE 5.1

Production Buyers	Number of costs	Retailers	Convergence	Number of stable states[a]	Price in a stable state[a]
Mobile	Equal	(1) Retailers choose among acceptable policies	Not ensured	—	—
		(2) = (1) + one cautious retailer	Ensured	Several	Single perfect competition price $(c+1)$
		(3) = (2) + one competitive retailer	Ensured	One	
Conservative	Equal	(4) = (1) + all 'learning' retailers	Ensured	One	Monopolistic price p^*
Heterogenous	Equal	(4)	Ensured	Several	Single or price dispersion
Mobile	Different	(2) The cautious retailer having the lowest production cost	Ensured	Several	Single
Conservative	Different Certain c_i's above p^*	(4)	Ensured	One	Price dispersion
	All the c_i's below p^*	(4)	Ensured	One	Monopolistic price p^*

[a] In this table, two stable states are considered identical if they are associated with the same price structure.

permit it—the rent associated with a monopolistic price. Should a competitive retailer arrive, the price will fall to the bottom.

Now, in reality, the same phenomena may be observed. Equilibria may be stable with a certain group of producers and cease to be so when certain producers change their conduct. The equilibria of traditional theory are merely borderline cases which are particularly robust but which assume, on the part of at least a minority of producers, adequate profit-searching behaviour. The analyses in this chapter thus allow us to come back to this fact drawn from experience: to be efficient a market economy does not assume only markets; it also implies behaviour patterns—that is to say, it requires the presence of adequate cultural factors.

6
The Revelation of Quality
Through Price

This chapter—the last in this first part—will deal with more subtle organizational properties of markets than the preceding ones. The best way to understand their nature is to start with the following apologue: a wine of either good or bad quality is brought to the market; certain agents know the quality, others do not; but the price which is established and which is dependent on the quality will nevertheless be the same as if all the agents were informed, since it allows the uninformed to deduce from it the quality of the wine and to act accordingly. In other words, the decisions of informed agents influence equilibrium prices in such a way that the latter reveal to the rest information which is held only by certain individuals.

The existence and uniqueness of 'revealing' equilibrium prices have been under study for twenty years or so by such economists as Akerlof (1970) Lucas (1972), Green (1972, 1977), Radner (1979), Grossman (1981), Milgrom and Stokey (1982), and a review of this literature was proposed by Jordan and Radner (1982). Laffont (1985) sums up the results obtained:

let m be the number of random variables (that is the number of real parameters which permit the description of the quality of goods)[1] and n the number of relative prices (that is the number of goods in monetary terms).[2] If $m < n$, there exist generically totally revealing equilibria. If $m = n$, there exist robust counter-examples of inexistence. If $m < n$, there exist equilibria with noise if one agrees to use very discontinuous price functions.

For those who have taken an interest in Shannon's information theory, these results are easily understood: prices, as channels of information, have a maximum capacity, they can as a general rule only transmit information whose variety is within that capacity.

---

[1] Parentheses added.   [2] Parentheses added.

Nevertheless, all the works which have just been evoked are limited to the study of equilibria. They do not deal with the dynamics of the transmission of information through price on a market other than in equilibrium or with the convergence or non-convergence of that market towards a fully revealing equilibrium.

That is the problem which will be the subject of this chapter. In keeping with the spirit of this book, we shall limit ourselves to the substance of things, the mathematical developments being reduced to a minimum.[3] Convenience leads us to examine successively:

- the presentation of the model;
- the results when the information on quality is complete;
- the results when the information on quality is incomplete.

The Model

The object is to study the dynamics of the market for goods, which, in the course of successive periods, might be sold at two quality levels, the quality being the same throughout one period but able to change from one period to the next. The sellers and some of the buyers know the quality from the beginning of the first period, while the rest of the buyers have no knowledge of it. The quality becomes public information at the end of a period.

Two examples may furnish a fuller understanding of the model. Sellers produce wine but during each period the quality depends on the climatic conditions. The sellers and informed buyers are able to infer the future quality of the product at harvest time while the uninformed buyers find out much later (once they have drunk the bottles of wine!). Alternatively, sellers distribute in a city handcrafted products from a poorly developed country; the quality of the product varies with the shipment. The sellers and informed buyers, with the help of tests, are able to evaluate the goods while uninformed buyers can only judge the quality after use.

The sets of buyers and sellers are invariant from period to period, each seller hoping to sell and each buyer to acquire one unit of goods per period. One quality is preferred to the other by the total set of buyers. The quality which appears at period t is random, but there exists a number T, such that over every group of T consecutive

---

[3] Readers who wish to do so may consult Laffond and Lesourne 1988, Laffond 1989.

periods both qualities are observed. In the course of each period, all the buyers will successively appear in random order once and only once on the market, but the order of appearance poses a problem to the uninformed buyers since they need to observe the transaction price to infer the quality of the product. Hence the need to consider at least two extreme hypotheses:

*P*1: the uninformed buyers begin to appear as soon as the first transaction has taken place and therefore mix with the informed buyers.

*P*2: the uninformed buyers only appear after the informed buyers and therefore constitute a second wave of buyers.

The uninformed buyer who appears on the market wants both to form a hypothesis on the quality of the goods sold and to acquire a unit of goods. What hypotheses can be formed on his behaviour?

• One might accept first of all that he observes at random a sample of transaction prices and compares the average observed to a reference price indicator of each quality; he then conjectures that the quality being sold is the one whose indicator is closest to that average.

• One might then assume that he draws a sample of sellers at random, contacts them one after the other in random order, makes them a price proposition, and stops the search as soon as a seller accepts his proposition. This proposition may be different (and a bit more favourable) for the buyer's privileged seller, if there is one— that is, for the seller from whom the buyer acquired a unit of goods during the preceding period; two modalities are conceivable in this respect:

• scenario V_1: the price proposition is only made to sellers still having goods to sell (which means that the sellers can only take into account the sales made);

• scenario V_2: the price proposition is made to any one of the sellers (which means that the sellers will take into account the offers received).

In like manner, each seller, at the beginning of each period, fixes a bottom price above which he will accept the buyers' propositions. The bottom price may be different (and a bit lower) for the seller's privileged buyer if there is one, that is to say, for the buyer to whom the seller sold a unit of goods during the preceding period.

When going from one campaign to another, the buyers revise their reference prices and their price propositions while the sellers adjust their bottom price:

● At the end of a period, the uninformed buyer learns whether the quality sold was good or bad and consequently compares the corresponding reference price to the average transaction price observed, making sure that the reference price for the best quality is never lower. Simultaneously every buyer adjusts his price proposition for the quality that has just been sold, improving it, but not beyond an upper limit—if he has not managed to buy—and lowering it except for the privileged buyer if he bought a unit of goods. A question then arises: does the buyer also modify his price propositions for the other quality? He knows, in fact, that the buyers uniformly prefer one of the qualities to the other. For simplicity's sake, we shall assume here that the buyers do not link the markets.

● As for the sellers, they take into account the fact that they have or have not sold a unit of the goods they possessed and the price propositions that they received, notably the maximum offer. When the bottom price is lowered, it never goes below a certain minimum and when it is raised it applies to all buyers except the privileged buyer.

As the preceding chapters have emphasized, the hypothesis, for the agents of a buyer or a privileged seller, is not without importance. Indeed, as all the buyers and all the sellers do not know each other, a stable state can only be established on the basis of permanent relations between buyer-seller couples, but first, for such relations to exist, the search for more favourable conditions must be carried out with agents other than the privileged agent.

All the values are in whole numbers—as is usual in these models—and adjustments are made in steps of one unit. A step thus represents both the price difference that an agent accepts for changing privileged partners and the variation of reserve prices between the periods.

In order to demonstrate correctly the role of the diverse hypotheses in the process of negotiation and the forming of expectations, it is desirable to examine market dynamics first when all the buyers are informed, and then when a fraction of them has no knowledge of the quality of the product.

The Dynamics of Complete Information

Introducing into the case of incomplete information the hypotheses *P*1 and *P*2 on the buyers' appearance obliges us to consider two reference cases when information is complete:

- a first situation in which the buyers appear in a wave, all the orders of appearance during each campaign having a non-zero probability of happening;
- a second situation in which the buyers appear in two successive waves, the order of appearance being random within each wave.

In the first situation, the market converges in finite time—under trivial hypotheses—towards a stable state which corresponds to the traditional equilibrium of elementary theory for each of the qualities. The 'demand curve' being obtained by classifying the buyers in decreasing order according to their ceiling price and the 'offer curve' by classifying sellers in increasing order of their minimal acceptance price. The various stable states are indistinguishable since they simply correspond to the different allocations of effective sellers to effective buyers for each quality. We shall designate by E_1 the set of these stable states.

Then there exists for each quality $\alpha(\alpha \in \{1, 2\})$, a price p_α such that the prices operating in a stable state be within $\{p_\alpha + 1, p_\alpha\}$ or $\{p_\alpha - 1, p_\alpha\}$.

In the second situation, the market also converges towards a stable state of E_1 when the buyers make propositions to any one of the sellers (scenario V_2). The sellers in fact then integrate the propositions of the second wave of buyers into the elaboration of their acceptance price, which avoids breaking the market up into two distinct markets, one for the first wave and one for the second.

On the other hand, in scenario V_1, the set of these stable states is made up of distinct states in which effective buyers and sellers are different, in which the prices are not so identical, and in which the buyers in the first wave obtain a lower price than those in the second for each quality. It is the random history of the market which determines the stable state that is reached.

We shall take E_2 to designate the set of stable states under these hypotheses (P_2, V_1). To explore the properties of E_2, a and b will denote the two waves, and we shall consider for a state e of E_2, the minimum price $p(a, \alpha)$ and the maximum price $\bar{p}(a, \alpha)$ paid in that state by a buyer of the first wave (we shall in like manner introduce $p(b, \alpha)$ and $\bar{p}(b, \alpha)$).

It is then easy to show the following four properties:

(i) $\bar{p}(a, \alpha) \leq \underline{p}(a, \alpha) + 1$ $\bar{p}(b, \alpha) \leq \underline{p}(b, \alpha) + 1$

In other words, in the same wave, the buyers pay (to a unit more or less) the same price.

(ii) $\bar{p}(a, \alpha) \leq \underline{p}(b, \alpha) + 1$

In other words, the price paid by the buyers of the first wave is always lower than that paid by the buyers of the second. A very normal result since the buyers of the first wave potentially address all the suppliers while the buyers of the second wave only have access to a restricted offer.

(iii) max $\{\bar{p}(a, \alpha), \bar{p}(b, \alpha)\} \geq \underline{p}_\alpha \geq$ min $\{\underline{p}(a, \alpha), \underline{p}(b, \alpha)\}$

In other words, the equilibrium prices $\underline{p}_\alpha$ fall within the interval of the prices operating in a stable state of E_2.

(iv) A state e of E_2 is a state of E_1 if, and only if, for each quality α, there exist on the market at the most two prices differing by a unit.

If there were buyers appearing now in the first wave, now in the second, the states of E_2 which do not belong to E_1 would disappear: indeed, by being incorporated into the first wave, the floating buyers would adjust to the low prices of that wave while buying a product (because some of them are efficient);[4] in changing over to the second wave they would adjust to these higher prices while allowing their privileged seller to receive price propositions from the buyers in the second wave; finally, coming back to the first wave, they would cause a rise in prices of that wave and so on until complete homogenization of the market is achieved.

The above analysis already sheds some light on the problem of revealing quality through price. Since the buyers prefer quality 1 to quality 2, $p_1 \geq p_2$ in equilibrium. What is more, we shall assume here that:

$$p_1 - 1 < p_2 + 1 \tag{1}$$

---

[4] In the sense cited in Ch. 3.

Under these circumstances, for an outside observer, the problem of revealing quality through price is resolved in every state in E_1 since condition 1 is always satisfied. It is not necessarily the case for a state in E_2. To demonstrate it we shall introduce the sub-set E_3 of E_2 states such that if supplier k sells his merchandises to an individual of the first wave, supplier k' who is less demanding follows suit. In other words, E_3 is the set of stable states in which the buyers of the first wave buy from sellers with the lowest acceptance prices.

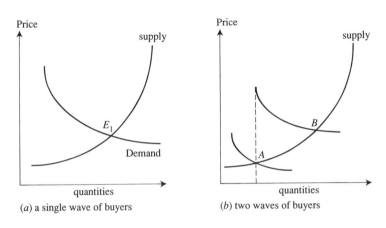

FIG. 6.1

Fig. 6.1 illustrates this situation:

- the graph on the left corresponds to the existence of a single wave of buyers; E_1 is the situation of traditional equilibrium and the purchases of E_1 differ only in the allocation of sellers to buyers;
- the graph on the right corresponds to the existence of two waves of buyers, the first wave of buyers has the least demanding suppliers as sellers and benefits from prices corresponding to A while the second wave of buyers is confronted with other buyers and pays the price corresponding to B; the set E_3 is represented by the two points of intersection A and B, the states in E_3 differ only by the allocation of buyers to sellers within each wave.

Put another way, everything happens as if, in a state of E_3, the buyers of the first wave address all the sellers. An equilibrium is established at a price $p\,(a,\alpha)$ such that every buyer of the first wave who does not buy has propositions $v(i,\alpha)$ below $p(a,\alpha)$, and every seller who does not sell to a buyer of the first wave has a reserve price above $p(a,\alpha)$. The buyers of the second wave then address themselves to the remaining sellers and a price $p(b,\alpha)$ is established.

It can be shown that:

- the states of E_3 are states of E_2 in which the buyers of the first wave pay the lowest price and those of the second wave the highest;
- the states of E_3 correspond to states of the market in which the surplus extracted by the first wave is a maximum.[5]

For an outside observer, the problem of revealing quality through price arises if, in a stable state, the price paid by buyers for good quality is lower than that paid by the buyers for poor quality.

Considering the characteristics of states in E_3, this could happen if:

$$p(a,1) - 1 < p(b,2) + 1 \tag{2}$$

Here we begin to see what will be the main result in the last part of this chapter. On the threshold of this section we shall limit ourselves to mentioning the relations, practically obvious, which exist between the three sets E_1, E_2, and E_3:

$$E1 \subset E2 \qquad E3 \subset E2 \qquad E1 \cap E3 = \varnothing \tag{3}$$

The Dynamics in Incomplete Information

When information is incomplete, a state of the market becomes a couple made up of a state of the market with complete information and the set of reference prices which uninformed buyers associate with the two qualities. In a stable state all the parameters are independent of time except the reference prices which may differ from one campaign to the next.

For set E_1, there is thus a corresponding set F_1 of stable states which are naturally revealers of quality since they correspond to traditional equilibria of elementary theory with informed agents. It is possible to show that the market converges in probability in finite time towards these traditional equilibria:

---

[5] In the sense defined in Ch. 2.

- when the uninformed buyers appear at the time of the first transaction (hypothesis *P*1);
- when the uninformed buyers form a second wave (hypothesis *P*2), but the sellers have access to all of the offers received (scenario V_2).

The first point of this proposition allows us to affirm that there are plausible market dynamics which lead simultaneously to price construction and the revelation of quality to uninformed buyers when the latter do not feel that, to improve their knowledge, they are obliged to wait until all of the informed buyers have made their appearance; when this is so, the uninformed buyers, in spite of their initial handicaps, do not experience any of the final disadvantages since they pay the same price as the others.

The second point considers the case in which uninformed buyers feel that to observe the market they must wait until the knowledgeable buyers have all made their appearance. In this situation also, there exist plausible market dynamics which lead simultaneously to price construction and the revelation of quality when sellers can receive offers from all of the buyers. This result stems from the fact that first wave buyers take the propositions of uninformed buyers into account in their decision; the uninformed may get the price message and, in the long run, pay the same price as the informed.

The case (V_1) $(P2)$ remains to be explored: the sellers are only sensitive to the transaction price; the uninformed buyers only appear on the market after the entry of the informed ones.

We can then define two sub-sets of E_2, E'_2, and E''_2 such that:

$$E''_2 \subset E'_2 \subset E_2 \tag{4}$$

E'_2 is the set of E_2 states in which the informed buyers pay a higher price for the good quality than they pay for the poor.[6]

E''_2 is the set of E'_2 states in which the prices operating reveal the quality to uninformed buyers. With $p_t(\alpha)$ and $P_t(\alpha)$ denoting the minimum and maximum prices obtained in a state for quality (α), the condition which is necessary and sufficient for that state to belong to E''_2 is that:

$$P_t(2) \le \frac{p_t(1) + p_t(2)}{2} < \frac{p_t(1) + p_t(2)}{2} < p_t(1) \tag{5}$$

---

[6] Leaving problems of unit aside.

Two situations may come about with respect to the relative positions of the preceding stable states. They are illustrated by Figure 6.2:[7]

1. If $E_3 \subset E_2''$, the quality is revealed to uninformed buyers, even when the informed buyers contract with the least demanding sellers. The market then converges in probability towards a stable state of F_2'' (the extension of E_2'' for the adding of reference prices). The

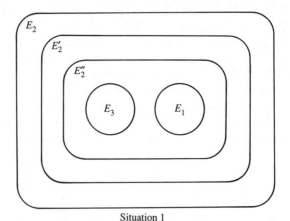

Situation 1

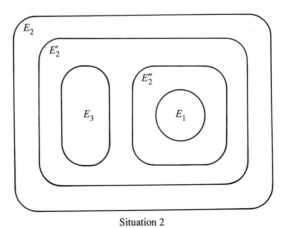

Situation 2

Fig. 6.2

[7] Intermediate situations are limited to specific cases of no general interest.

stable state attained by the market depends on its history and even if the uninformed buyers discover the quality, they must accept less favourable prices than those obtained by the informed buyers, the price difference being in a way the penalty they must pay for discovering the quality.

2. If $E_3 \cap E_2'' = \varnothing$, the quality is not revealed to uninformed buyers in E_3 states. Then the market does not always converge towards a stable state and does not necessarily reveal the quality. It may in fact, as time goes on, either end up in a stable state of E_2'', or irreversibly enter a set A of unstable states, the uninformed buyers never succeeding in deducing the quality from the transactions observed.

It is easy to see how this situation comes about: in the course of a period, the informed buyers (wave a) enter the market first and offer price $p(a, \alpha)$ to their privileged sellers who accept it; the uninformed buyers enter in a second wave (wave b) and their higher offers are not taken into account by sellers who have sold to buyers of the first wave, since these suppliers are only sensitive to the sales prices. Nor can the other suppliers modify market stability in the first wave because their minimal pretentions are above the informed buyers' offers (at level $p(a, \alpha)$). From there on, for each quality, the markets for the two waves of buyers follow independent courses. The market for the first wave remains stable and its state reproduces itself identically from one period to the next. The market for the second wave fluctuates unendingly. In their search for the best price, the uninformed buyers lead prices towards levels such that revelation of the quality is no longer ensured: seeing that they are in error, these buyers permanently search for information and that search destroys the convergence towards a single price.

Conclusion

The message of this chapter can be contained in a few lines: the same limited rationality behaviour may lead the market either towards a stable state in which prices reveal quality, or towards an indefinite run of fluctuations. Uninformed buyers search for the best price and, at the same time, information on quality. When the market does not furnish them with this information they put off their entry. By so doing, they leave informed buyers the time to organize their purchases and search out the best opportunities. In a good many cases, this behaviour is justified, since, outside of traditional equilibrium, no situation is granted and irreversible for the informed buyers. In other cases this behaviour succeeds partially: informed buyers organize their purchases around prices which reveal the quality to uninformed buyers, but the latter must accept higher prices. Finally, there is one last eventuality: the efforts of the uninformed buyers fail, the dual aims of searching for the minimum price and for information on quality prove to be incompatible, and the market fluctuates indefinitely with multiple transaction prices.

Thus, through contacts among agents, the market reveals capacities of self-organization which are both far reaching and imperfect, far reaching because they are not limited to constructing prices, imperfect, because, in certain circumstances, convergence towards stability may be broken or stability might not engender a single price.

Comments on the First Stage

At this stage of analysis, four conclusions may be drawn:

1. There is no need for an auctioneer. For the market to sort out supply and demand and to make itself into an organized whole, it is sufficient that economic agents make random and sequential contacts and that their behaviour presents a certain degree of coherence.

Our research does not yet allow us to give a general definition of the minimal coherence. It does, however, make possible a rough sketch of its contents: the nearly exclusive use of information obtained through individual research, recall of the recent past and a few more distant events, perseverance in the effort to improve the situation, the revision of demands in order to take past errors into account, and the safeguarding of acceptable situations.

2. The emergence of a market as an organized whole is thrice costly to the agents: it demands of them time or expenditures for obtaining information; it is carried out on a more or less long horizon; and it takes the market through numerous more or less organized intermediary states.

Thus the processes which ensure both the revelation of price (and possibly of quality) and the double dichotomy of offers and demands are by nature 'imperfect'. Consequently, there appear multiple equilibria with price dispersion, which may differ according to the agents carrying out the transactions on the market. Indefinite fluctuations without convergence are equally possible.

In other words, the market of elementary micro-economic theory constitutes a borderline case, like the reversible transformations in thermodynamics. In reality market dynamics are irreversible; they end up at best in a state of partial organization.

3. The multiplicity of the stable states means that the final state depends both on the initial state and on the random historic path of the markets, and, as a consequence, the two economic systems which are identical and in the same state S_0 at the initial moment,

will be found, at a certain horizon T, to be in two distinct states S_t^1, and S_t^2 and thus, beyond T, will not have the same perspectives for change. In particular, the prices certain agents are faced with in T may allow the development of a new activity for one system and rule it out for another. The differentiation which has come into being between 0 and T has become irreversible.

4. The stable states, when they are multiple, do not all have the same robustness. A number of them owe their existence solely to the passiveness of certain agents: the absence of a supplier with competitive behaviour makes possible the perenniality of a price level ensuring the sellers a rent; the limiting of search efforts to a minimum by all the buyers allows the sellers to operate a monopolistic price; the coexistence of active and inactive agents breaks up single prices. The stable states with little robustness—which might be called stable states of surfusion—are in no way a theoretical curiosity. In practice they play a considerable role: in developing countries, where the operation of markets does not conform to the prognostications of neo-classical theory because cultural habits engender less enterprising behaviour; in certain regions or certain branches of industrial countries neglected by the most active agents, where the existence of rents upstream in a line of development hinders the birth of activities downstream. Thus, a market at its borders may be, by the properties of its dynamics, a facilitator or an inhibitor.

But it may also, and this will be the theme of Part II, through self-organization, give rise to a whole range of institutions. In this sense it is worthy of being termed a creator.

Part II
The Market as Creator

7

The Birth of Intermediaries

Any market, even if its fundamental parameters are constant, remains in a situation of disequilibrium as long as convergence to a stable state has not been attained. Very often, this stable state is itself very sensitive to the particularities in agents' behaviour. Hence the possibility of new actors appearing who will try to take advantage of market dynamics or statics for personal ends and in this way contribute to accelerating the convergence to a stable state or to slowing it down by destabilizing the market.

This chapter will deal with the birth of two categories of this type of actor:

- recruitment agencies which contribute to improving the operation of the labour-market;
- speculators who, depending on the case, can reduce or raise the variability of market prices for durable goods.

The biological analogy in Chapter 2 which pointed out the similarities betwen the formation of a cellular membrane and the setting of a price, helps us to understand the appearance of these intermediaries. Some have an interest in protecting the membrane or accelerating its construction, others in destroying it or hindering its formation. The same intermediary can, moreover, depending on the circumstances, cross over from one category to the other without ceasing to follow the same objectives.

The Appearance of a Recruitment Agency

This problem will first of all be studied in the context of the labour-market model with the information costs given in Chapter 3, assuming the parameters of this market to be stable. It will, secondly, be examined in a larger framework against the variation of the parameters of a single market or the coexistence of multiple markets associated with different skills.

A recruitment agency on a single market (with constant parameters)

Let us start with a banal observation: as long as the labour-market is not in a stable state, there are individuals who do not find jobs which interest them and firms which do not detect applicants whom they could recruit.

This being the case, as economists have been writing for two centuries, possibilities for earnings open up to agents able to obtain information under preferential conditions and to sell it to other actors present on the market.

But how can a recruitment agency actually appear?

1. First of all an individual—who may not be one of the operators on this labour-market—must discover the imperfection in the functioning of the institution and invent, through imitation, analogy, or creation, the activity which will allow him to take advantage of this imperfection.

2. It is then necessary for this individual to have access to a specific technology which will give him competitive advantages over the others.

3. Thirdly, it is indispensable that the individual deem the prospects for future earnings satisfactory if he should enter the market. For this reason he naturally considers:

- the cost he must accept for his agency to be made known to a worker or a firm;
- the costs of collecting information at each period and the nature of the information obtained;
- the price that he hopes to operate and the number of clients he hopes to obtain at each period;
- the decrease in the sum the agents will normally be willing to pay as the market progresses towards equilibrium.

Thus the birth of an intermediary does not only result from the objective dynamics of the market. It also depends on the creativity, the technical capacity, and the way anticipations are formed by the eventual participants. In societies where the spirit of enterprise is developed and this type of activity valued, recruitment agencies may appear even though the mathematical expectation for profit is negative. In other societies, on the contrary, notable earning prospects do not motivate an entry on to the market.

Let us now assume that an agency has been created. We shall try to describe the consequences for the evolution of the labour-market, and to do so we shall return to the model with information costs in Chapter 3. In this model, worker k decides whether or not to draw, in the second sub-period of period t, on a sample of jobs in order to be able to enrol on the lists of applicants for period $(t + 2)$ and eventually to find employment for period $(t + 1)$. The worker's choice stems from a comparison of costs and anticipated income in the various solutions, c_k designating the costs of drawing a sample and $\alpha_t(k)$ the intrinsic value of market observation. It is convenient to let the individual observing have the probability ε of discovering any one of the jobs.

This is where the agency comes in: for cost a, it is able to detect every post with probaility η. It offers this service for price d. The existence of the agency, its fee, d, and the number, η, are common knowledge. Under these circumstances, a worker has the choice of one of four strategies:

- not to search and not to buy the agency's services (cost 0);
- not to search and to buy the agency's service (cost d);
- to search and not to buy the agency's services (cost c_k);
- to search and to buy the agency's services (cost $c_k + d$) (in this last case, the probability of discovering any one of the jobs is $\varepsilon + \eta - \varepsilon\eta$).

If υ is the number of individual buyers, the agency's benefits during period t are obviously $(\upsilon d - a)$.

What is the effect of the agency's presence on market evolution and, in return, the influence of the market on agency policy?

1. Let us begin by assuming that the agency's fee is constant. If d is very low, its amount is inferior to the maximum value $\bar{\alpha}_k$ which every individual associates with observation. In other words, the presence of the agency transforms all individuals into active individuals who search, sooner or later, and the market tends towards a concentrated and efficient stable state. Convergence is also quicker than in the absence of an agency.

If one increases parameter d, the number of individuals who have permanent recourse to agency services diminishes and as certain

$\bar{\alpha}_k$'s fall below d, the corresponding individuals adopt a passive attitude while stable states with wage dispersion appear.

At any rate, when the market approaches stability, the number of individuals who have an interest in buying agency services should—according to mathematical expectations—decrease, along with the agency's hopes for profit per period.

Let there then be an agency, created with financing T, which must accept an initial investment I, and which operates the constant fee d. Leaving discounting aside, its finances at the end of period τ are the random variable:

$$T_\tau = T - I + \sum_\tau^1 (v_t d - a) \tag{1}$$

Under these conditions, the agency may have several histories:

● If—once the market is in a stable state—the number of individuals having recourse to agency services for guidance on the market is sufficient, the benefits from operating the agency will remain positive and the agency will come to coexist permanently with a market in equilibrium.

● If—a second possibility—future benefits:

$$\sum_\tau^\infty (v_{t'} d - a)$$

—at a date inferior or equal to the date of convergence—appear to the owner of the agency to be insufficient for justifying continued activity, the agency's existence will be transitory, due to the voluntary ceasing of activity during the evolution of the market.

● There is, finally, a third possibility: chance may cause the agency to find jobs of little interest to its clients; they may turn away from it prematurely, and agency funding may be annulled at date t. The agency would then be forced to end its activity even if hopes of future benefits were satisfactory. This agency's existence would be transitory due to a financial crisis.

The incidence of one or other of these developments is conditioned by all of the following:

● the givens of the market structure (bottom and ceiling price of both workers and firms);
● the parameters characterizing an individual's search for information (information costs, maximal values attached to observation, the probability of discovering a job);

- the permanent elements particular to the agency (investment costs, operating costs, the probability of discovering jobs, available funds, rules of conduct);
- the conjunctural events resulting from the randomness of market evolution.

2. But, naturally, the agency will modify d as the market moves towards convergence. It finds itself in fact faced with a demand curve $v_t(d)$ which it knows imperfectly. It only knows:

- that given t, the number of clients decreases when its fee increases;
- that when t increases, the number of clients decreases on the average at a given fee.

We must be careful not to conclude too rapidly that the agency will constantly reduce its fee as the market converges because it is less advantageous for the workers to make use of its services. In fact, at a certain point, it may be in the agency's interest to concentrate solely on a clientele of active individuals, giving up that of transitory searchers. Logically, the agency should then operate a fee which maximizes its receipts from active individuals.

Naturally, in reality, the agency will explore the effects on its income of a rise or reduction in its fee based on an initial rate chosen according to its anticipations. Thus a recruitment agency's entry on to the market engenders two consequences:

- it reduces the mathematical expectation of convergence time;
- it increases, if the agency does not close beforehand, the number of active individuals and eliminates the stable states with high wage dispersion.

Nevertheless, if one is limited to the foregoing description, the existence of intermediaries would seemingly have to be most often transitory. This is not the case at all, for obvious reasons which will now be considered.

The perenniality of recruitment agencies

A glance at the French economy is enough to see that recruitment counselling agencies are doing very well. Such longevity is easily interpreted from a theoretical point of view, two types of model, which are actually complementary, being available to us.

1. Hypothesis one: the recruitment agency only operates on a single labour market, but the structual parameters of this market are continually submitted to discontinuities: the arrival or departure of workers, the entry or exit of firms, technical innovations modifying the firms' ceiling price, and modification of individual attitudes towards work. The result is that the market starts off in search of a new stable state before having attained one of those towards which it was converging. In other words, it is permanently in a situation of disequilibrium, which allows the agency to see its possibilities for profit rebuilt.

Thus, the intermediary is an economic agent whose profitability—and therefore survival—subsists on the perenniality of disequilibria in the market. If one qualifies the agents operating on the market as agents of the first rank, the intermediaries appear as agents of the second rank whose existence is linked to operating imperfections and shocks undergone by the market. These agents of the second rank may themselves give birth to a market, the labour-market of the professionals in recruitment, with the emergence of agents of a third rank: the offices specializing in recruitment for recruitment agencies. This hierarchical vision is, however, too rigid since, in practice, agents of different rank recruit on the same market.

2. Hypothesis two: the recruitment agency is interested in several independent markets at various stages of their evolution. From time to time new markets are created while others reach equilibrium or disappear. Under these conditions, the agency permanently redistributes its activity, eventually pulling out of markets approaching equilibrium and giving priority to action on new markets.

This analysis raises two points:

• The markets' constant but disturbed search for stable states evokes the notion of equilibration introduced by Perroux in 1975 in order to describe situations of broader scope than situations of equilibrium.

• The existence of agents whose perenniality depends on an average amount of market disequilibrium explains in part the social resistance governments run into when they try to reduce these disequilibria (in order to fight inflation, for example). Such actions do indeed economically condemn to death at least a fraction of the intermediaries. The strategies of the intermediaries introduced up to this point result in improvement of market operations. Naturally this is not always the case.

The Emergence of Speculators

This problem is as old as the science of economics. As early as 1789, it drew the attention of Adam Smith in his famous *Inquiry into the Nature and Causes of the Wealth of Nations*. A distinction should be drawn, however, between speculators who transmit no false information and destabilize the market by simply using available information and those who intentionally disrupt the market by taking advantage of the diffusion of inexact information.

1. In the first instance, I shall draw inspiration from the recent analysis by Hart and Kreps (1986) because it brings out perfectly the phenomena which interest me.

I shall consider the market for stockable fungible goods, such that during each period t there is time to reach equilibrium price p_t. The demand comes from two categories of agents:

- consumers who buy the goods for immediate use (the quantity they demand $q(p_t, \theta_t)$ depends on price p_t and a random income parameter θ_t with identical and independent distributions which can take on two values $\underline{\theta}$ and $\bar{\theta}$);
- speculators who eventually acquire goods to stock them for a period and to resell them at the next period (they can stock, at the most, a quantity K notably inferior to the total offer).

In every period, the offer is constant and equal to Q (naturally not counting the quantities resold by the speculators).

There exists, in addition, public information ξt which gives the speculators an indication of the future parameter θ_{t+1} defining consumer demand: ξ_t can take on two values $\underline{\xi}_t$ and $\bar{\xi}_t$. When ξ_t is observed, the speculators know that future consumer revenue will be modest ($\theta_{t+1} = \underline{\theta}$); when $\bar{\xi}_t$ appears, they know that there is a low probability ε that future consumer revenue will be high ($\theta_{t+1} = \bar{\theta}$).

Let us now assume that demand functions, in order to simplify things, have the following properties:

- for $\theta_t = \bar{\theta}$, the demand is perfectly elastic for a very high price p_1;
- for $\theta_t = \underline{\theta}$, the minimum price is p_2, the demand falls to the Q level when the price rises from p_2 to p'_2 and becomes perfectly elastic in p'_2 which is a low price level. On such a market, two prices reign in the absence of speculators:

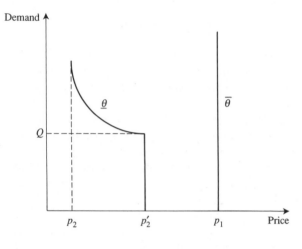

Fig. 7.1

- the price p'_2 which is low when $\theta_t = \underline{\theta}$;
- the price p_1 which is high when $\theta_t = \bar{\theta}$.

What conduct do speculators adopt in the four situations with which they may be confronted?

(i) For $\theta_t = \underline{\theta}$ and $\xi_t = \underline{\xi}$, the speculators do not buy, since the current price is at least equal to p_2 and the future price does not go above p'_2, and is hence an insufficient return on investment.

(ii) For $\theta_t = \underline{\theta}$ and $\xi_t = \bar{\xi}$, the speculators buy quantity K; in fact, by behaving in this way, they do not raise the current price above p_2 and have the probability of ε selling at price p_1, and hence should be sure of earnings, even with a low ε, should p_1 be well above p'_2.

(iii) For $\theta_t = \bar{\theta}$, the current price is too high for speculators to buy whatever ξ_t may be. What effect, then, does the presence of speculators have on the price?

- If $\theta_t = \bar{\theta}$, the price remains equal to p_1, even if the speculators put quantities which they bought in $(t - 1)$ on the market.
- If $\theta_t = \underline{\theta}$, two eventualities must be considered:
- $\xi_t = \bar{\xi}$, the speculators acquire K on the market, leaving $Q - K$ available to consumers, but this does not bring on any change in the price which remains equal to p'_2;
- $\xi_t = \underline{\xi}$, the speculators do not buy; but they sell K if they had bought in the preceding period, that is to say, if $\theta_{t-1} = \underline{\theta}$,

$\xi_{t-1} = \bar{\xi}$; in this eventuality their behaviour brings on a drop in the price to a level p_2'' situated between p_2 and p_2'.

To conclude: in the presence of speculators the price fluctuates between p_2' and p_1 and consequently shows greater variability. This result is obviously not valid for all values of the parameters. The speculators' entry on to the market might very well express itself in a reduction of the range of price variations.

As for the appearance of speculators, it assumes the uniting of conditions very similar to those described for the recruitment agency:

- the presence of individuals capable of interpreting the message ξ_t and imagining the activity of buying and reselling;
- the possibility for these individuals to have access to a satisfactory stocking technology;
- the existence of prospects for future earnings deemed acceptable by these individuals if they should enter the market.

2. I shall now turn to the circumstance in which disruptive agents consciously transmit inexact information.

To do so, I shall come back to the labour-market with information costs and I shall assume this market to be in a stable state. When this is so, the set of individuals is doubly divided: first into groups of employed and unemployed individuals, secondly into passive and active individuals. The latter periodically search for jobs which might interest them, see that they have not found any, and keep the job they have.

But let us now imagine the appearance on the market of an agent who transmits anonymous information on the wages in operation. This agent assures the individuals of the existence of jobs offering higher salaries and leads some of these individuals to search for other employment while raising their demands; at the same time he tries to convince the firms of the existence of individuals receiving lower wages and incites a fraction of these firms to lower their propositions. Under these conditions, the stability of the market is disrupted if certain individuals quit their jobs as soon as they are refused a rise in salary and if certain firms fire their workers rather than continue paying the same wages. Once the market is disorganized, it becomes more difficult for the actors to discover the inaccuracy of the information initially communicated to them. The disruptive agent can then offer his services in recruitment assistance, but in so doing he draws the market closer to stability. He must therefore continue to spread rumours in order to slow down convergence even while he contributes to it. One understands how interesting theoretical analysis of such dynamics would be, but it seems a priori to be relatively delicate.

Economists have long known that certain markets are more easily penetrated than others by these disruptive agents. Manuals frequently cite a stock exchange as an example. Several factors do indeed make disruption of the stock market relatively easy: for example, the unending changes in prospects for growth in enterprises, the uncertainty of these prospects, the lack of confidence certain actors have in their anticipations, the possibility for actors to be either buyers or sellers, the absence of intrinsic value of the goods exchanged, the perenniality of the goods, the low transaction cost, and the role of prices in revealing information.

The disruptive agent's manœuvre is of the simplest sort and Braudel (1979) cites examples on the London Stock Exchange which go back to the seventeenth century. First, the agent circulates false information on the prospective profitability of the industrial and commercial operation which sustains particular transferable securities. In this way he influences the anticipations of some of the actors and brings prices down. He then enters the market as a buyer and patiently waits for new information to correct the rumour, send prices back up, and allow him to make a substantial profit.

Thus the market mechanism, as described in the first part of this book, is likely to engender actors other than the primary actors on the market, actors who can be called intermediaries.

When intermediaries are but simple, facilitative instruments, they may reveal through their appearance the creative properties of the dynamics of disequilibrium, but have only limited influence on the future. It is already a different story when, behaving, voluntarily or not, as disrupters, they modify the price chronicles of transferable securities and in this way are capable of encouraging firms to abandon or to go through with investment projects. They then contribute to the irreversibility of economic changes.

Inasmuch as the market contributes to making new actors appear whose influence is persistent, it can be termed a creator. But the next few chapters will show us that the preceding process is only one of the processes of creation which are associated with the market mechanism.

8

The Forming of Opinions

Twice already, the role of opinion forming in market dynamics has appeared in this book: in Chapter 3 when the workers, in the presence of information costs, accepted being unable to hope for revenues superior to those observed in the past, and in Chapter 6 when the individuals, faced with goods of unknown quality, used prices to form an assumption on the quality of the goods.

Nevertheless, in both cases, the creating of opinion did not make up the central element of the hypothesis. It will be entirely different in this chapter which deals with the influences that individuals exert on their respective opinions: direct influences resulting from contacts, and indirect influences resulting from parallel efforts to interpret price formation.

Devoted to direct influences, the first part of the chapter will treat mimetic phenomena, assuming that, after a number of random, successive meetings, economic agents modify their opinions as they take others' opinions into account.

In dealing with indirect influences, the second part of the chapter will be a study of the creation of stable states whose characteristics confirm the agents in a common belief which is objectively unfounded. The specialist will recognize, in professional jargon, the equilibria with sunspots.

At this point, the reader might legitimately wonder why this chapter figures in the second part of the book. The answer, I believe, will become clear as the arguments are developed, but a rough outline is already possible: market dynamics may contribute to the elaboration by the individuals of a representation of the world which, once diffused and standardized, will constitute a collective norm of belief influencing the course of real economics.

Mimesis

For this analysis of the economic significance of mimesis, I propose a five-step process; after a description of the simplest phenomena of mimesis, those which introduce imitative individuals, I shall illustrate the description with a brief presentation of two models from David (1988) and Kirman (1988), and take up the mimetic phenomena which involve anticipative individuals. Finally I shall consider, following Orléan (1989), individuals who take into account simultaneously their own observations and the opinions of others.

1. A model by Laslier (1989) perfectly illustrates the mechanism of evolution in opinions based on imitation: the individuals n in number ($1 \leq i \leq n$) estimate at $x(i, t)$ the value that they attribute during period t to one particular commodity. In the course of this period, an individual i (the contacting individual), drawn at random according to a uniform law, meets another individual j (the contacted individual), also drawn at random according to a uniform law. These two individuals communicate their evaluations and revise them according to the information obtained.

Naturally, the rules of revision cannot be the same depending upon whether the evaluations are free or constrained.

Let us say first that they are free. Various means of re-evaluation are imaginable:

- the first individual chooses $x(i, t + 1)$ by a uniform drawing out of $[x(i, t), x(j, t)]$ or $[x(j, t), x(i, t)]$, the other individual not being influenced;
- the two individuals modify their estimations, either independently of each other, or by agreeing on an intermediary estimate or by each taking a step towards the other.

It can then be shown that given t increasing indefinitely, all individuals agree on the same value for the goods; that value cannot be foreseen in advance since it depends upon history.

On the other hand, what about the case in which evaluations are constrained, each individual i only accepting a revision of his estimation within the interval $[w_i, v_i]$?

In this case two outcomes are possible:

- if the intersection of individual intervals is not empty, the estimations tend towards a common value belonging to this intersection;

• if the intersection of individual intervals is empty, either there is no absorbent state in the process and estimations fluctuate indefinitely, or there is an absorbent state and estimations converge towards set individual values, but remain distinct.

In spite of their simplicity, the preceding mechanisms play a preponderant role in certain economic or political situations. Thus it is often considered that those involved in a financial market belong to two groups with distinct behaviour patterns: the 'fundamentalists' who think values are determined by fundamental economic variables and the 'chartists' who consider that these values evolve in an autonomous manner. Now, a market on which only 'chartists' were to be found would be run by a mechanism dependent solely on the evolution of opinions.

Another related illustration concerns a government's putting shares of a state-owned company in the course of privatization on to the stock market. While awaiting a price announcement, the operators try to estimate the value of the stock. Initially the evaluation made by each operator is founded on relatively objective data (the characteristics of the company and its perspectives) and on some which are less objective (reflections on the political conjuncture, for example), but during the period of time which separates the announcement of the project from its realization, the operators communicate among themselves and in one way or another modify their evaluations.

We might also have a look at the spreading of a rumour peddled throughout the population by individuals in no way committed by the rumour in question: two stable states are then conceivable depending upon whether the rumour dies out or is taken as truth by the whole of the population.

Lastly, we can mention the forming of voting intentions prior to a referendum, the individuals, decidedly for or against from the start, drawing to them variable respective proportions of the undecided.

At this point, two particular models—each with its own added value—will allow us to carry on with our analysis.

2. The first (David 1988) was inspired by the apologue by Schelling in *Micromotives and Macrobehaviour* (1978). In its original form, it deals with the co-ordination of behaviour, but it is easy to reinterpret it in terms of opinion diffusion.

A slow, steady snowfall covers a shop-lined street in the centre of a town. The section of sidewalk in front of each shop can remain practicable if, from time to time, the shopkeeper goes out to clear it. But a shopkeeper considers that shovelling the snow off is in his interest if, and only if, the sidewalk of at least one of the two adjacent shops remains practicable. Each shopkeeper observes the situation periodically and adopts the following empirical rules for making a decision depending upon his observations:

- if the sidewalk in front of the two adjacent shops is clear, he clears his part;
- if the sidewalk in front of the two adjacent shops is piled with snow, he will leave his portion of the sidewalk as it is;
- if the sidewalk is cleared on one side only, he will clear his portion, again with the probability $p(0 < p < 1)$.

It is clear that the evolution in the policy of each shopkeeper is represented by a Markov chain while the collective conduct of the shopkeepers on the street follows a stochastic process made up of independent Markov chains and positive local feedback. This process has two corresponding absorbent states:

- one with a total absence of collaboration among the shopkeepers—in this state the snow piles up on the whole length of the sidewalk;
- the other with complete co-operation among the shopkeepers—in this state, the sidewalk is regularly cleared off by the whole group of shopkeepers.

The same model could inspire an apologue on the evolution of beliefs: in an imaginary country, during a revolution, some shopkeepers—opportunists—put a flag up in their shops if they believe in the victory of the insurgents and take it down if they think the government will win. In the absence of other information, they form an opinion by observing their neighbours' behaviour. Two flags? They get out or keep theirs. Only one flag? They foretell events at random. No flag? They cautiously refrain from showing one.

A more economic illustration would be to assume that shopkeepers must form an opinion on the opportuneness of putting up a window display with advertising material which they are not sure will be well received by the clientele.

The preceding model is a particular example of models known in statistical physics under the name of Ising models. These models describe systems of particles, oriented in space, which modify their orientations in relation to that of their neighbours. This representation therefore leads to a space of phases with a complex but calculable geometry, with multiple valleys of potential separated by barriers. The system can therefore easily be trapped in states which are only local minimums of potential.[1]

These models are interesting to economists because, for systems with local interactions within a network, they lead to equilibria which are path dependent.

3. The second example will be borrowed from Kirman (1988). In a text entitled *On Ants and Markets*, Kirman takes a look at *N* economic agents divided up into two groups differing in their beliefs. At each period, two agents, chosen at random, meet, the first having the probability:

- $(1 - \varepsilon)$ of adopting the beliefs of the second;
- $\varepsilon/2$ of changing groups;
- $\varepsilon/2$ of staying in the group he belongs to.

This formulation differs from that of Laslier since the agent can modify his belief without any influence from his fellow agent.

By taking k to designate the size of the first group ($1 \leq k \leq N$), the above process may be described by the transitions:

$$k + 1 \text{ with the probability } [1 - k/N][\varepsilon/2 + (1 - \varepsilon)k/(N - 1)]$$
$$\nearrow$$
$$k$$
$$\searrow$$
$$k - 1 \text{ with the probability } [k/N][\varepsilon/2 + (1 - \varepsilon)(N - k)/(N - 1)]$$

If one excludes extreme cases ($\varepsilon = 1$, no interaction, and $\varepsilon = 0$, the first individual adopts the beliefs of the second), the distribution of the size of the first group is given for N increasing indefinitely by the relation:

$$f(x) = \lambda x^{\alpha - 1} (1 - x)^{\alpha - 1}$$

with $x = k/N$ and $\alpha = \varepsilon N/2$

The function f corresponds to a symmetrical distribution β whose form, which depends on α, is recalled in Figure 8.1. When α is such

---

[1] An introduction to the study of the Ising models can be found in Green and Hurst (1964), Fisher, Grinstein, and Khurana (1988), Sompolinsky (1988).

that we find ourselves in case (*a*), the economic agents may for a certain time share the beliefs of the first group, then convert— slowly at first, then rapidly—to the belief of the second. Hence the random shift with time from one major belief to another major belief.

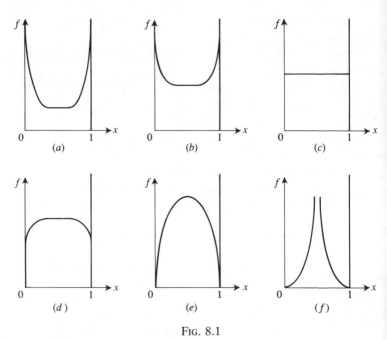

FIG. 8.1

Kirman applies the preceding model to a foreign exchange market in which two groups of 'fundamentalists' operate. According to the first group, the evolution of the exchange rate s_t during period t tends to draw it towards the value s_1. The group consequently forms the forecast:

$$s_{t+1}^1 = s_t + v_1 (s_1 - s_t) \tag{1}$$

v_1 being a constant characteristic of this group. The second group for its part reasons on the basis of value s_2 and elaborates the prognostication:

$$s_{t+1}^2 = s_t + v_2 (s_2 - s_t) \tag{2}$$

From there on, if w is the percentage of agents belonging to group 1, the forecast which will govern the evolution in the exchange rate will be given by the relation:

$$s_{t+1}^* - s_t = wv_1(s_1 - s_t) + (1 - w) v_2(s_2 - s_t) \tag{3}$$

Under these conditions, if w is governed by a stochastic process of form $(1 - a)$, evolution in the exchange rate will sometimes be governed by relation (1) and sometimes by relation (2) with a random shift from one to the other.

Case (b) leads to similar phenomena. In cases (c) and (d), there is never a belief shared by a majority. Finally, in cases (e) and (f) a stable dominant belief prevails.

Thus, even in the simplest form, phenomena of mimesis can have a profound influence on the evolution of an economy. By standardizing the beliefs, by contributiong to the formation of groups with distinct opinions, they can, depending on the history, engender profoundly different states.

4. But there do exist instances of mimesis which are more complex than the preceding ones: they are those in which individuals, through their faith in the information gleaned from contact with others, try to anticipate the value of a variable along the lines of the model of evolution of the variable they believe in.

Thus Laslier (1989) studied a process in which individuals, convinced that the value of a commodity increases linearly with time, anticipate the value at the following period by using information communicated by others in the past. In other words, all the actors believe in the validity of a model of the form '$at + b$' with coefficients a and b to be discovered.

The individuals—n in number—supposedly have a memory of finite dimension T and the initial state of the system is defined by the nT estimations $x(i, u)$ of the first T periods $(1 \leq i \leq n, 1 \leq u \leq T)$. At period T, each individual i linearly adjusts vector $[x(i, 1), \ldots, x(i,T)]$ over vector $[1, \ldots T]$ and gets a relation $x = a_i t + b_i$ which he uses to obtain his forecast for period $(T + 1)$:

$$\hat{x}(i, T + 1) = a_i(T + 1) + b_i \tag{4}$$

The individuals then communicate these forecasts through a process of random bilateral contacts. More precisely, for each individual i, an individual $J(i) = j$ is uniformly drawn at random out of $\{1, \ldots, n\}$ and for date $(T + 1)$ i adopts the estimation:

$$x(i, T + 1) = \sigma x(j, T + 1) + (1 - \sigma)\hat{x}(i, T + 1) \tag{5}$$

in which $\sigma(0 \le \sigma \le 1)$ is a parameter of the model common to all the individuals. The procedure is then repeated from period to period.

Now what can be demonstrated? The following result: if all the individuals believe in a linear evolution in relation to time of the real value of the estimate, they implicitly end up by agreeing on the parameters a and b of that evolution and by forming identical estimations in every period.

Thus the model, representative of the generating of evaluations, which they shared at the beginning is confirmed through mimesis, though it corresponds to no prior reality, and its parameters are collectively determined, their final value a_∞ and b_∞ depending upon the history of contacts.

But what happens to this result if a fraction of the population does not believe in the existence of a linear trend and adopts through imitation the following rule of estimation: 'tomorrow's value will be the average of what it was at the last T dates'? It is profoundly changed since the simple presence of a non-zero fraction (even a small one) of imitative individuals is enough to make the forecasts for t sufficiently large, identical, and constant. In other words individuals, whatever their number, who assume that a is null impose their point of view on the whole group of fellow citizens. They force anticipative individuals to revise their estimation of the coefficient of the trend $a(i, t)$ down to zero. Naturally, the final common value b_∞ depends on the series of meetings.

5. Finally, we shall introduce individuals who take into account simultaneously their own observations and the opinions of others.

Orléan (1989) considers a share, the fundamental value of which is a random variable V liable to take three values a, b, and c with probabilities $p, 1 - 2p, p$ ($p < 1/2$). He admits, to make computation easier, that:

$$a = b - \delta \qquad c = b + \delta \tag{6}$$

Time being a discrete variable, he assumes that a new agent arrives on the market immediately after the beginning of every period. This agent then chooses irreversibly his expectation, taking into account two sources of information:

- the real distribution of the random variable V (therefore he draws at random a sample in the theoretical 'urn' associated to V and consequently obtains a with probability p, b with probability $(1 - 2p)$, and c with probability p);
- the distribution of opinions of the agents already present on the market, represented by the vector which is common knowledge, of the proportions of agents having respectively selected expectations a, b, and c:

$$x_t = \{ x_a(t), x_b(t), x_c(t) \} \tag{7}$$

The agent considers he has to deal with two risks: the one due to the natural randomness affecting the fundamental value and the one 'related to the fact that, for unforeseen reasons, an investor, to meet unexpected circumstances, may be compelled to sell his portfolio'.

The second risk, which Orléan calls competitive, is proportional to the square of the difference between the chosen expectation i ($i = a$, b, or c) and the average evaluation. Hence:

$$r(i, x_t) = [i - (ax_a(t) + bx_b(t) + cx_c(t)]^2 \tag{8}$$

The choice of the investor may then be described in the following way: he must make a trade-off between the loss of anticipated gain resulting from the fact that he selects i instead of the value drawn from the urn j and the decrease in the competitive risk which derives from his choice. In other words, we may assume that the agent selects, for j given, the expectation i which minimizes a function of the type:

$$c(i, x_t) = |i - j| + \mu r(i, x_t) \tag{9}$$

μ being a trade-off coefficient.

It is then possible to prove that, given t increasing indefinitely, vector x_t converges towards a fixed vector of final proportions of opinions a, b, and c. Depending on the agents' random drawings and hence on the history of the process, the fixed vector is one of the six following:

$$
\begin{array}{ll}
B_a \ \mathbf{x} = (1, 0, 0) & S_1 \ \mathbf{x} = (p, 1 - p, 0) \\
B_b \ \mathbf{x} = (0, 1, 0) & S_2 \ \mathbf{x} = (0, 1 - p, p) \\
B_c \ \mathbf{x} = (0, 0, 1) & N \ \mathbf{x} = (p, 1 - 2p, p)
\end{array}
$$

N corresponds to the trivial situation in which the diversity of opinions reproduces exactly the distribution of the share fundamental value. B_a, B_b, and B_c describe three situations in which agents agree respectively on values a, b, or c. B_a and B_b imply important financial 'bubbles', i.e. differences between the expectations' average and V's mathematical expectation. These bubbles are equal to δ. Finally, S_1 and S_2 correspond to intermediate situations in which the diversity of opinion does exist but is less dispersed than V, the bubbles being equal to $p\delta$.

But all these final solutions are not simultaneously valid. As $\mu\delta$ increases, the normal solution N is progressively replaced by the solutions of unanimity as indicated in Table 8.1. Thus 'the mimetic process generates, as soon as the randomness of the phenomenon considered becomes too big, a diversity of opinions smaller than the one which would prevail in situations currently described by economic theory. Such dynamics may even lead to situations of unanimity. Generally, these situations imply financial bubbles, the opinion unanimously accepted differing from the expectations of the fundamental value.'

TABLE 8.1

Value of $\mu\delta$	Final state
$\mu\delta < 1/(1+2p)$	N
$1/(1+2p) < \mu\delta < p$	N, S_1, S_2
$p < \mu\delta < 1/(1-2p)$	S_1, S_2, B_a, B_b, B_c
$1/(1-2p) < \mu\delta$	B_a, B_b, B_c

This analysis sheds light on the role played by mimetic phenomena in the forming of opinions. But this analysis runs up against its own limits: by restricting its horizon to direct influences, it excludes from its field the interactions which are conveyed by observations of the market. A hypothesis from which the second part of this chapter is free.

The Generating of Sunspot Equilibria

Since the time of Azariadis (1981) and Azariadis and Guesnerie (1982), a step has been made towards understanding how there can be 'self-fulfilling prophecies', that is to say, how the announcement of certain forecasts makes them come true.

Let us recall the context in a few words: an economy whose life extends through a series of periods unites a constant population of individuals of overlapping generations who live two periods each. During the second (old age) they can only consume and must therefore during the first period (youth) earn their living and save for their old age. But the amount of savings depends on their anticipation of the future prices of consumer goods.

It has long been known that, under certain hypotheses, such an economy has a permanent system of equilibrium prices as well as the behaviour of young and old being identically reproduced from period to period.

But let us now suppose that, at each period, the individuals observe the random presence or absence of sunspots. These spots have no influence on conditions of production in the economy, but the individuals are convinced that they will influence prices. If we then take A to designate the presence of a sunspot at a given period and B its absence, we can show that for a supposedly single consumer good there exist individual price anticipations, p_x and p_y, which are produced when event A or B occurs. Hence, the possibility of equilibria with sunspots—that is, equilibria characterized by forecasts which prove to be true even though at a collective level they have no objective basis.

However, this theorem of existence does not enable us to understand how these equilibria are created. It says nothing of how individuals can induce their observations from forecasts creating at their own instigation behaviour which progressively gives birth to the prices anticipated in the presence or absence of sunspots.

Hence the interest in thinking about the dynamic processes that, starting with any individual forecasts, through self-organization lead to the emergence of stable states whose properties depend on the appearance of sunspots.

To do so let us consider (Laffond and Lesourne 1989) an economy with overlapping generations in which:

- the individuals live two periods with the same number n of young and old agents in each period;
- there are only two goods, the currency whose mass M is constant over time and a non-stockable commodity whose life span is limited to one period.

During his youth (period 1), an agent receives as remuneration for his work an endowment T of consumer goods. He consumes part of it Q_1 and exchanges the rest Q for cash. During his old age (period 2), he exchanges his stock of cash for a quantity Q_2 of consumer goods. If p_1 and p_2 designate the respective prices of these two periods:

$$Q_2 = (p_1/p_2)Q \tag{11}$$

It is assumed that the agent's utility is expressed by:

$$U = \min(Q_1, Q_2) \tag{12}$$

In other words, the agent seeks to maximize his minimum consumption over the two periods.

We shall in turn devote our attention to the existence of equilibria, stationary or not, to the dynamics of an economy when the agents believe in the influence of sunspots, and to the origin of the development of that belief.

1. The preceding economy is liable to have stationary and non-stationary equilibria.

A stationary equilibrium is characterized by a price p^*, such that, when the agents anticipate the renewal of this price from period to period and determine their behaviour in consequence, this price is actually established.

It is easy to show that in the case examined there is but one single equilibrium associated with the price:

$$p^* = 2M/nT \tag{13}$$

each agent consuming $T/2$ over each of the two periods of his existence.

But, in a more general manner, one may wonder under what conditions a series of prices $\{p_t\}$ can engender a succession of non-stationary equilibria. A simple demonstration—which the reader will be spared—allows us to affirm that any series $\{p'\}$ proving the relation:

$$p_t p_{t+1} / [p_t + p_{t+1}] = M/nT \qquad (14)$$

defines a sequence of these equilibria.

2. We shall now introduce individual expectations and the dynamics which result from them.

At the start of each period t, every young agent $i(i \leq i \leq n)$ formulates the expectations $\hat{p}_t(i)$ and $\hat{p}'_t(i)$ for the price of the consumer goods in period t and $(t + 1)$. He deduces his behaviour from them for period t, and the market of that period rapidly evolves towards a stable state characterized by price p_t observable by all agents at the end of the period.

To start with, suppose that the individuals, conscious of the permanent character of the economic structures, find it normal to make the same price expectation for two successive periods $(\hat{p}_t(i) = \hat{p}'_t(i))$. Let it also be accepted that every young agent i of period t has a son, and only one, in the following generation, a son who can also be designated by the symbol i and to whom he transmits the price he observed and his expectation. This son then formulates for periods $(t + 1)$ and $(t + 2)$ the expectations:

$$\hat{p}_{t+1}(i) = \sigma_i p_t + (1 - \sigma_i)\hat{p}_t(i) \qquad (15)$$

in which $\sigma_i(0 < \sigma_i < 1)$ designates a smoothing coefficient which is also handed down identically from generation to generation.

On the basis of the preceding hypotheses it can easily be shown that whatever the initial distribution of the expectations may be, such an economy converges towards a single stable state which is no other than a stationary equilibrium. In this state all the individuals correctly anticipate the equilibrium price p^*.

The reader may find rather artificial this lineage of individuals who hand down preferences, information, expectations, and smoothing rules from father to son. Other scenarios are obviously possible: there is nothing to keep us from assuming, for example, that an individual lives indefinitely, alternating seasons of work and free time (without transmitting a heritage of a two-season cycle to the one who follows).

Let us now change the agents' representation of the world: from here on they are convinced that sunspots influence the course of the economy. To put it another way, at the beginning of period t, the young individual of rank i anticipates respectively:

- the price $x_t(i)$ for all the periods with sunspots (mode A);
- the price $y_t(i)$ for all the periods without sunspots (mode B).

The linking of these events in period t is then as follows:

- the observation of the mode of the period (A or B) by all the individuals;
- the choice of the quantities to sell by the young individuals;
- the setting of the market price and the execution of transactions;
- the transmission of price expectations to the future generation.

The agents know the random conditions of the appearance of sunspots. More precisely:

- if mode A prevails in period t, they know that modes A and B will appear in period $(t + 1)$ with the respective probabilities α and $(1 - \alpha)$;
- if mode B reigns in period t, they know that modes A and B will occur in period $(t + 1)$ with the respective probabilities β and $(1 - \beta)$.

Consequently, when, in the presence of A, a young individual chooses Q, he does so by maximizing the utility he hopes for:

$$U = \alpha U_A + (1 - \alpha) U_B \qquad (16)$$

with $U_A = \min \{T - Q, Q\}$ and $U_B = \min \{T - Q, [x_t(i)/y_t(i)]Q\}$

In this relation U_A and U_B denote the utilities obtained when modes A and B appear respectively in the course of period $(t + 1)$.

A simple calculation then shows that individual i's optimal decision consists in making the following choices:

$\alpha < 1/2$ $[x_t(i)/y_t(i)] < \alpha/(1-\alpha)$	$Q = T/2$
$[x_t(i)/y_t(i)] > \alpha/(1-\alpha)$	$Q = \{y_t(i)/[x_t(i)+y_t(i)]\}T$
$[x_t(i)/y_t(i)] = \alpha/(1-\alpha)$	Q lies in the closed interval of the two preceding values.
$\alpha > 1/2$	$Q = T/2$
$\alpha = 1/2$ $y_t(i) < x_t(i)$	$Q = T/2$
$y_t(i) > x_t(i)$	$Q \quad \{T/2,[y_t(i)/(x_t(i) + y_t(i))]T\}$

A similar calculation allows us to determine individual i's decision when he is put in the presence of mode B, α being replaced by β.

As for the expectations, they are adjusted as follows: when mode A has appeared in period t, agent i's heir revises the expectation relative to that mode in keeping with the relation:

$$x_{t+1}(i) = \sigma_i x_t(i) + (1 - \sigma_i)p_t \qquad (17)$$

and keeps the expectation relative to mode B constant:

$$y_{t+1}(i) = y_t(i) \tag{18}$$

The adaptation is symmetrical when it is mode B that has prevailed in period t.

What are the stable states of the preceding dynamics? The answer to this question is highly interesting.

1. If at least one of the probabilities α or β is greater than 1/2, the only stable state is the stationary equilibrium with prices independent of sunspots:

$$x = y = 2M/nT \tag{19}$$

2. If the two probabilities α and β are less than 1/2, all the states characterized by prices x and y and verifying the following necessary and sufficient conditions are stable:

$$\begin{cases} \alpha/(1-\alpha) < x/y < (1-\beta)/\beta \\ xy/(x+y) = M/nT \end{cases} \tag{20}$$

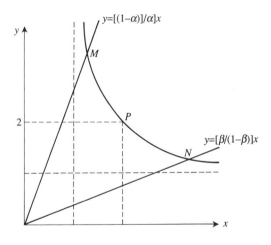

FIG. 8.2

Fig. 8.2 which has been drawn with units chosen so that $M/nT = 1$ shows the geometric locus MN of the equilibria; among them is the stationary equilibrium P. Moreover, whatever the initial distribution of expectations the state of the economy converges in finite time towards one of the stable states MN.

The stable state attained depends on the initial opinions and the history of sunspots. According to this history, the individuals' self-occurring forecasts associate the appearance of sunspots with a high price ($x \leq y$) or a low price ($x \geq y$) for the consumer goods.

But what happens if there exists in the population a stubborn individual who absolutely denies the influence of sunspots? The answer should not be surprising: he wins the others over as in the case of the linear anticipations above. His behaviour suffices to destroy the stability of all the states of MN except the stationary equilibrium P.

3. This result naturally leads to a new question: how can individuals be led to believe in the theory of the influence of sunspots?

To try to answer this question, we can assume that at each period t, every young individual i has a choice between two conceptual models of economic operations:

- the model which denies the influence of sunspots;
- the model which confirms this influence.

The choice is governed by a number $\delta_t(i)$ which represents the individuals' degree of belief in the validity of the first model:

- if $\delta_t(i) \geq 1$, the individual behaves as if the first model were true;
- if $\delta_t(i) \leq 0$, the individual adopts the second model;
- if $0 < \delta_t(i) < 1$, the individual draws his 'explanation of the world' at random with the probability $\delta_t(i)$.

When the individual rallies to the first model, he sells the quantity $T/2$, since he anticipates the same price over periods t and $(t + 1)$. When he adopts the second model, he follows the optimal rules of decision calculated previously. At any rate, after observing the actual prices of period t, the individual—or rather his heir—refigures his expectations $x_{t+1}(i)$, $y_{t+1}(i)$, and $\hat{p}_{t+1}(i)$ and modifies his degree of belief:

- to $\delta_t(i) + \varepsilon$ with $\varepsilon > 0$ if the price observed is closer to the postulated price without the influence of sunspots than to the supposed price with this influence;
- to $\delta_t(i) - \varepsilon$ in the opposite case.

But at this stage, two sets of hypotheses are conceivable:

(i) The individuals adopt a definite belief as soon as $\delta_t(i) \geq 0$ or $\delta_t(i) \leq 1$. If $\delta_t(i) \geq 1$, they deny for once and for all the influence of sunspots; if $\delta_t(i) \leq 0$ they thereafter adopt the spot theory whatever their future observations may be.

(ii) The individuals continue to adapt $\delta_t(i)$ in relation to their observations, even if the degree of belief falls outside the open interval $]0, 1[$.

In the first eventuality, the process converges in probability towards a stable state in finite time: in that stable state the individuals all have the same belief as to the interpretation of the world; they have either definitively rallied to the theory of the influence of sunspots or they flatly deny the validity of the theory.

What is more, these two outcomes can be generated from the same initial state of expectations and degree of belief (at least if $0 < \delta_0(i) < 1$ for every i). Here is matter to open up new horizons.

In the second eventuality, on the contrary, the convergence ends up in a stable state in which the individuals unanimously reject the sunspot theory.

But even if the belief in sunspots has disappeared in the end, in the course of dynamic change, this belief may have deeply influenced the behaviour of the real economy.

Hence the conclusion: in every economy, the processes of opinion-forming, whether they create transitory or definitive, true or false beliefs, modify the production and allocation of goods. The science of economics has a socio-psychological dimension impossible to overlook.

The Beginnings of a Theoretical Understanding of Economic Development

It would be easy to criticize the brief nature of certain models in this chapter and notably the dynamic model in the second part. Such criticism would, however, miss the essential, since it would neglect the fundamental contribution represented by this dawning of an understanding of the role played by the creating of opinions in the processes of economic self-organization. One can indeed imagine that, in more complex models, the interaction between the forming of beliefs and the dynamics of the real economy would not simply have the effect of modifying the chronicle of change in a consumer price, but would deeply transform the course of the economy as a whole, sending it off on different trajectories as concerns the amount and use of savings. Thus, in spite of their insufficiency, the models in this chapter begin to reconcile micro-economic theory and the practitioners' vision of development. The latter, indeed, never cease to emphasize the historic and global character of development. Historic, because the development of a society remains to a certain extent unpredictable. Global, because it brings aspects into play which are at the same time cultural, economic, and political. It is perhaps only a trace, but history and culture are present in the theoretical analyses in this chapter.

9

The Creating of Skills

This chapter, using a particular case, takes up a major question: how can the very operations of an institutional structure (in this case, a market) give birth to a new structure (in this case, two markets)?

The particular case examined is a labour-market in which all the workers are unskilled. At the outset, there is then just one labour-market. However, when certain workers are employed by certain firms, they can acquire technicians' skills. As the firms have the choice between systems of organization calling for either workers or technicians, a second labour-market of variable size is liable to appear. Depending on history, the economy will use the whole of its human resources, transforming into technicians all the workers capable of being so, or will ensnare itself in a final state rendering a greater or lesser fraction of its human capital unproductive.

Once the model and its dynamics have been outlined, the chapter will deal with the properties of stable states and pose questions concerning the contribution this analysis may make to the understanding of economic phenomena.

A Dual Learning Model

The characteristics of this model can be summed up in a few lines:

• Initially, all the individuals have the same professional skills (skill level 1), but a few of them will have the chance of acquiring higher skills (skill level 2).

• Initially, all the firms offer only skill 1 jobs (corresponding to the use of a simple technology, technology 1), but they may also eventually propose—either having known about it all along or discovering it by chance—a more elaborate technology calling for an individual with skill level 2 (technology 2).

● A skill level 2 individual can accept either skill 1 or skill 2 jobs.

● Contrary to the model in Chapter 2, it is now the firms which enter the market at random and randomly attract individuals. At each period, a firm sets the salaries it will offer for jobs in technology 1 or technology 2. The individuals declare themselves applicants or not, and the firm adopts either job vacancies due to lack of applicants, the only way open to it if there are no applicants for one of the organizations, or the most profitable of the two organizations if it has a choice.

It is useless to go back over the process of adaptation of individual wage demands and firm offers: they are modelled upon those described in Chapter 2. On the other hand, attention should be given to the dual learning phenomena.

For the individual learning process, several hypotheses illustrating the different aspects of reality are conceivable:

1. Each individual k has a probability p_k—which may be zero—of being changed into a skill level 2 worker through training during any one work period. Being immediately informed, he can during the following period apply for a skill level 2 job.

2. The preceding probability does not depend solely on the individual but on the firm i as well (it is not the same thing to be recruited by IBM as by a modest resale firm in information technology products). From there on, the individual only progresses, basically by chance, if he encounters a firm likely to train him. Consequently the model involves probabilities p_{ki}.

3. For an individual–firm couple, the learning probabilities are effective only in the individual's first employment period with the company; the individual's abilities are fixed thereafter. What is more, a 'transformed' individual can only eventually apply for a skill level 2 job in another firm if the firm responsible for the change actually decides to make use of the individual's level 2 skills by adopting technology 2.

A similar range may be offered concerning hypotheses on company training:

1. Every firm knows both technologies from the start and, from the first period on, investigates the benefits of adopting one or the other.

2. A firm initially only knows technology 1, but, during any

period in which the job is held, it has the probability Π'_i—which, moreover, may be zero—of discovering technology 2.

3. A firm initially only knows technology 1, but during any period in which the job is held by a skill level 2 individual (either company trained or an outsider), it has the probability Π'_i of discovering technology 2. Thus in this case it is capable individuals who make it possible for the company to discover the existence of a more complex and often more profitable technology.

Whatever the junction of learning hypotheses, the market converges—which is no surprise—to a stable state, but the diverse stable states may prove to be quite different: while in some states numerous firms will be satisfied with using a primitive technology and employing unskilled labour, in other states, most of the firms will opt for the complex technology with the use of skilled labour. Hence the interest in examining these stable states in more depth.

Properties of Stable States

To facilitate the analysis it is convenient to specify clearly the learning hypotheses. For that reason, we shall assume hereafter that the firms know both technologies from the start and that every individual k of skill level 1 has the probability p_{ki} (which may be zero) of being transformed into a skill 2 individual during any one work period with firm i.

All individuals being originally at skill level 1, it is normal to call:

- a promotable individual, any individual k for whom there exists a date t and a succession of non-zero probabilities of market states $e_0, e_1 \ldots e_t$ for which this individual will have acquired skill level 2;
- a promoted individual, any promotable individual for whom there exists a date t' at which this individual has acquired skill level 2 as a result of the effective functioning of the market.

M_p will denote the set of promotable individuals, but depending on the stable state attained, the set of promoted individuals will not always be the same.

To compare the market evolution to a reference situation, imagine a market identical to the foregoing one but such that originally the individuals in M_p are already at skill level 2 and those in $M - M_p$

at skill level 1. This market will converge to a stable state, but the diverse stable states will be indistinguishable, the individuals employed being the same for each skill level and the jobs held identical as well as the technologies they require. M_e will denote the set of employed individuals (individuals said to be efficient by convention) in any one of these stable states. We know that, in these stable states the surplus is maximum, the market making full use of available sources of manual labour.

Let us come back to the functioning of the market with learning. We shall say that this mechanism ends up in a complete stable state if this stable state is such that all the promotable, efficient individuals ($k \in M_p \cap M_e$) have been promoted. Under these conditions, the market mechanism has revealed all of the usable learning potential which existed in the economy. It has generated no waste of human resources.

But there naturally exist incomplete stable states.

When the market converges to one of these stable states, the economy, from a certain date on, has been trapped in an evolution which has made a part of its potential human resources unproductive.

With every state of the market e_t, we can associate a surplus S_{e_t} defined by the relation:

$$S_{e_t} = \sum_{i \in N_t} \bar{v}_{\alpha_t(i)} - \sum_{k \in M_t} w_k \tag{1}$$

where Mt and Nt are respectively the sets of individuals hired and jobs filled, the revenue, not counting salaries, of firm i when it uses technology α_t at period t, $\bar{v}t(\alpha_t \in \{1, 2\})$ and w_k individual k's minimum wages.

It can easily be shown that:

(i) if e_1 and e_2 are two stable states and M'_1 and M'_2 the sets of promoted individuals in these two states then:

$$M'_1 \subset M'_2 \text{ implies } S_{e_1} \leq S_{e_2} \tag{2}$$

(ii) if e_1 is a stable state and e_3 a transient state in which the set of promoted individuals is the same then:

$$S_{e_1} \geq S_{e_3} \tag{3}$$

It results that in a complete stable state the surplus attains its maximum maximorum.

But under what conditions are all the stable states in an economy complete?[1] This a difficult question and we shall limit ourselves to two particular cases:

- that in which all firms provide training (in other words, if for an individual k there is a firm j such that $p_{kj} > 0$, then for every other firm i, $p_{ki} > 0$);
- that in which all individuals are promotable.

Case one: all firms provide training

Consider the individuals employed in a job at skill level 2 in a complete stable state of the economy. We shall denote as m^*, the number of these individuals and as k_{m^*} the one among them with the greatest demands. If this individual and all those with high demands lost the possibility of being promoted, we should observe stable states where the number of individuals employed in jobs at skill level 2 would be $(m^* - 1)$. Then let:

$$s^1_{\min} (m^* - 1)$$

be the minimum of the equilibrium wages observed for employment at skill level 1.

It is then possible to show that a sufficient condition for all states of equilibrium to be complete is that:

$$s^1_{\min} (m^* - 1) \geq \underline{w}(k_{m^*}) \tag{4}$$

In other words, the most demanding of the employable individuals in a complete stable state must be both promotable and willing to work in a job at skill level 1 if he has not yet been promoted. Thus, when all firms provide training, it suffices, for the market to lead to full use of human resources, that the individuals not hinder their training by premature demands.

Case two: all individuals are promotable

In this second case, a sufficient condition for all stable states to be complete is that, in every complete stable state, there be at least one firm providing training which uses technology 1.

This firm will work for the collectivity by training individuals for skill level 2 until the stock of promotable, efficient individuals has been exhausted. Consequently, it is essential that all firms

---

[1] This is expressed in simplified form. It leaves aside the fact that, in a stable state, wages for the same skill level may differ by a unit (see Laffond and Lesourne 1985).

with in-service training have no interest in prematurely adopting technology 2.

These two particular cases help us to understand the nature of the mechanisms which, during the random functioning of a primary market, may give birth to secondary markets of variable importance, allowing a more or less efficient use of the potential resources in the economy.

In spite of its simplicity, the model which has just been analysed is absolutely essential to our understanding of economic phenomena.

A New Look at Economics

To speak of a 'new look' may seem excessive, but the expression is at least partially justified by the multiplicity of reflections to which the model may lead depending on whether we take the point of view of resources or technology, of institutions or growth, of industrial economies or developing economies.

1. If we set apart the well-known article by Arrow, 'The economic implications of learning by doing' (1962), and its descendants, the common practice in economic theory is to assume that resources are given or intentionally produced by the firms. In this model, on the contrary, the resources partially result from random events provoked by encounters among the actors during the exchange process. When this is the case, their creation is no longer ensured and the economy, depending on its past, actually transforms a variable fraction of its initial potential. The evolution may be blocked if the firms make too quick a rush for new resources or if the initial resources likely to be transformed are too costly.

2. But the appearance of new resources also means the development of new technologies. What the model points out is that the future position of these technologies is not given, since their profitability depends on the relative scarcity of the resources generated by market dynamics. In particular, the more the number of technicians increases, the more the equilibrium wages tend to decrease and the more the elaborate technology tends to spread at the expense of the initial technology.

In reality, this phenomenon may in addition be combined with the learning effect proper to technology brought out by Arthur (1989). The latter is interested in competition between two technologies *A* and *B*. At a moment of time, t, $n_A(t)$ and $n_B(t)$ denote the number of agents having adopted the first or second of these technologies respectively. During the following period, a new agent makes the irreversible decision of adopting one of these technologies. This agent may randomly belong to one or the other of two categories *R* and *S*. The revenue which his decision will procure him is shown in Table 9.1 with $a_R > b_R$ and $a_S < b_S$.

TABLE 9.1

Agent	Technology *A*	Technology *B*
Agent *R*	$a_r + rn_A$	$b_r + rn_B$
Agent *S*	$a_s + sn_A$	$b_s + sn_B$

Three situations are possible:

- There are no economies of scale in adopting a technology ($r = s = 0$); in this case the *R* agents always choose technology *A* and the *S* agents technology *B*. Each of the two technologies takes that share of the market which a priori suits them best.
- It is all the more interesting for an agent to adopt a technology as it becomes widespread ($r > 0$, $s > 0$); in this case, as t increases indefinitely, one of the technologies will dominate and from date t onwards will be adopted by all the agents. It is impossible to know beforehand, however, which of the two technologies will win out, the order of decisions of agents *R* and *S* playing a crucial role.[2]
- It is all the more interesting for an agent to develop a technology that is less widespread ($r <$, $s < 0$); in this case the outcome is foreseeable, neither one of the technologies will dominate on the market, and their respective shares tend towards a proportion which can be calculated.

In this model, the random nature of the order in which agents *R* and *S* enter the technology market renders uncertain—at least for a positive *r* and *s*—the result of a conflict between the technologies. It

---

[2] The existence of scale effects may come either from learning phenomena in the production, exploitation, or maintenance of equipment using the technology, or from the necessity of an infrastructure linking the equipment proper to this technology. In such a case, the collectivity may judge it necessary to define standards imposing technology *A* or technology *B*.

is on the contrary the encounters between workers and firms which have a determining influence in our model. Nevertheless, in both cases, it is random dynamics which give birth to an irreversible structure.

3. A third way of analysing the model is to study it from the institution point of view. Initially, the only institution is the market of workers: an institution which functions without an auctioneer thanks to contacts between firms and workers. The conjunction of these contacts and the possible transformation of the skills of certain individuals will suffice, with no outside intervention, to give birth to a second institution, the market of technicians. In other words, we have here an example of the endogenous birth of one institution as a consequence of the functioning of another. This second institution does not result from the will of any actor, it is the product of the actors' normal behaviour within the framework of a first institution.

Nothing stops us, moreover, from assuming that with the two technologies we will wind up with different products. If this is so, in the course of time, along with the labour-market for technicians, a market for product 2 will develop.

It would naturally be absurd to try to reduce to the mechanism brought out in this chapter, the entire morphogenesis of economic institutions. This morphogenesis is rich and varied as the remainder of the book will show and the contemporary science of economics is far from having identified all the types of linkages which lead to new institutions.

4. The fact that an economy is locked into a stable state rendering part of its potential resources unproductive may have more far-reaching consequences than simply the respective size of the two labour-markets. There is a good chance of the eventual appearance of innovations which, to be implemented, will require a sufficient number of 'technicians'. If the economy does not have this number at its disposal, it will have to give up adopting these innovations. It is well known, for example, that a country with only a handful of engineers or scientists cannot nurture hopes of developing—or even using—certain new technologies. But if such is the case, the difference between two economies identical at the outset becomes quantitative at a first stage (by variation of the number of technicians and workers respectively), and then qualitative at a second stage (by the possibility of access or non-access to certain classes of

innovations). The model in this chapter gives us a glimpse of the possibility of cumulative changes which place further and further apart economies having the same prospects for growth at the start.

5. Although the model may have been built essentially for theoretical reasons, the results obtained lead us to wonder whether the functioning of the labour-market in industrial countries, and particularly in France, might not be of a nature to render unproductive a part of the potential skills of its manual labour.

For this to be so, certain professional skills would have to be unobtainable through the educational system, and acquired only by experience. Thus, if the regulations concerning minimum wages and the right to work push the cost of unskilled labour (skill level 1 in the model) up to such a level that it generates classical unemployment, it is possible that young individuals, who would have been capable of acquiring professional skills giving them access to parts of the labour-market where there was full employment, may be excluded from all recruitment for a period of time which would eliminate the eventual possibility of promotion. This was very probably the case in France in the 1980s.

6. The problem of training is even greater in developing countries than in industrial countries. This training is very often acquired within certain firms, for example at the time when new factories are established. As a consequence of the small number of firms with in-service training, there is a great risk of a dysfunctioning of the labour-market expressed in the unproductiveness of human resources. Such is the case, for example, when the advantages that firms with in-service training offer the workers at skill level 1—advantages in the form of wages higher than those on the market—keep these workers from ever quitting their jobs. In fact, the firms, in this case, keep level 2 individuals on in level 1 jobs and do not contribute to the permanent training of technicians for the whole of the economy. This problem is clearly linked to that of the choice of industrial investments and production technologies. Heavy investment based on capital-intensive technologies often results in the creation of a small number of well-paid jobs with training. Hence the blockages that keep that industry from generating human resources for the whole of the economy.

These few indications suggest that, outside its immense theoretical interest, the study of self-organization phenomena may lead to the raising of highly pertinent questions of economic policy.

The model which has just been discussed belongs to the family of models in which the state of the market influences the fundamental parameters of economies. As a postscript to this chapter, it seems to me of interest to outline another model from this family whose object is to analyse the forming of consumer habits.[3]

In this model, exchanged, from period to period for monetary payment, are two commodities, the quality of which is constant through time and known to all. The sellers of the two goods are distinct, they each dispose of one unit and are individually characterized by a bottom sales price fixed in time. The buyers are indifferently interested in the two goods and consider them imperfect substitutes. Each buyer i is characterized at time t by two ceiling prices $\bar{v}_i(1, t)$, $\bar{v}_i(2, t)$ associated with the two goods. These prices vary in relation to past consumption, since past consumption supposedly influences preferences. In the course of a period, buyer i draws a sample of sellers for one or other of the goods, and decides to declare himself a taker of a unit of the commodity for which the difference between the ceiling price and the price offered by the seller is greatest.

The originality of the model lies in the link it establishes between the commodity α_t ($\alpha \in \{1, 2\}$) eventually consumed at period t and the ceiling prices $\bar{v}_i$ (α, $t + 1$) of the following period. Several hypotheses are conceivable: (1) the consumption of a good creates a habit and increases its desirability; (2) the consumption of a good temporarily reduces its desirability as the individual seeks variety; (3) the consumption of a good engenders an attitude of rejection which permanently diminishes its desirability.

We can imagine that the dynamics of such a model might take very different forms in relation to the distribution among the individuals of the various possible links between consumption and preferences.

Even if this model has the disadvantage of fusing into one set of dynamics the rapid dynamics of market convergence and the slow dynamics of the forming of habits, it presents the tremendous advantage of putting the accent on one of the motivating forces behind economic change, the interaction between transformations in production and change in tastes.

[3] On this subject, but in a wholly different context, see the article by Day (1986).

10

The Founding of Unions

Considering the importance of the role played by the labour unions in matters of employment, there is no reason to be surprised at the rapid development which micro-economic analysis of union behaviour has experienced (Farber 1986). The research has especially concerned the models in which the size of the union is predetermined, the aim being to explore the influence of union goals and the nature of wage and employment negotiations. Even in the more recent texts treating the size of the union as a variable, the models bring together a single enterprise and one set of workers and place themselves within the static framework of contracts theory.

In this chapter, however, emphasis is placed on the forming of the union as a constitutive element of the dynamics of a labour-market. The frame of reference remains that of Chapter 2, the market brings together individuals with identical professional aptitudes, each one offering a unit of work but differing in the minimum wages that they demand, and firms, each needing a unit of work from the preceding individuals but differing in the maximum salary they are willing to pay. Except for one technical hypothesis,[1] the given data define equilibrium wages in the absence of a union and we know that, under rather general conditions, the state of the market converges to a stable state in which the salaries are equal—to the nearest unit—to equilibrium wages.

But what happens to the preceding dynamics when a labour union is founded?

To study this question, I shall assume that throughout the life of the market, there exists one and only one potential union, for example an individual who is inoperative on the labour-market

---

[1] The existence of an individual and a firm such that the minimum wage of the first be equal to the maximum wage of the second.

under consideration, but who proposes to the workers that they join him in the creation of a union. I shall in turn deal with:

- the evolution of the market in the presence of this budding union;
- the perenniality of the union.

Finally, in the third part, I shall draw from this example a few reflections on the conditions necessary for the appearance of other institutions.

Evolution in the Market in the Presence of a Budding Union

Market dynamics can now be described with the following linkages:

1. During each period, a contract is offered each of the workers by the budding union. Under the terms of the contract, the worker commits himself to working only for firms that will sign with the union. Each worker naturally makes the decision to accept or refuse the contract after due consideration of his past experience and present information. The set of workers having accepted (if the set is not empty) constitutes the union at that period.

2. On the strength of the number of members and the commitments they have made, the unions announce to each firm a wage demand σ_t, at least equal to the equilibrium salary s_0. It is accepted that in the first period $\sigma_1 > s_0$, but the union disappears if the environment forces it to bring its demands down to the s_0 level.

Each firm is free to accept or refuse the union's offer on the basis of its past experience and its present information. It knows in particular that, if it rejects the union propositions, all the members will refuse to work for it. Thus a set is formed (which may be empty) of firms which have contracted with the union.

3. Each contracting firm draws at random the workers that it employs from among the members; this defines for each union member a probability of employment. We might also assume that— like bargemen navigating in turn—the members are recruited according to their order of arrival, that order varying randomly from period to period. We are therefore looking at a closed shop situation in which the union designates the workers that the firms should employ.

4. The non-members (if there are any) and the firms having rejected the union propositions (if there are any) find themselves on

the free labour-market confronting their reciprocal demands. A single salary s_t is rapidly established on this market and may be observed by all the actors.

Two markets then coexist in all periods:

- an organized market at salary level σ_t on which operate the set N_t of firms having signed with the union for period t and the set M_t of individuals who are union members (m_t and n_t will designate the cardinals of these two sets);
- a free market at salary levels s_t on which operate the other firms and other individuals.[2]

5. At the end of the period, the individuals and the firms, considering their recent experience, adapt their propensity to join the union or contract with it. As for the union, it will take into account the salary proposed during a period and its consequences in order to set the salary offered in the following period.

After this overall description of the functioning of the market it is proper to specify the behaviour of the individuals, the firms, and the union.

Individual behaviour

During period t, individual k will be characterized by the degree of appeal the union holds for him $a_t(k)$, the past and present level of which will determine his behaviour:

(1)   if $a_t(k) \leq 0$, the individual will not join the union;
(2)   if $a_t(k) < 0$ and:
  - $a_{t-1}(k) \leq 0$, the individual joins the union with the probability $p(k)$ ($0 < p(k) < 1$);
  - $a_{t-1}(k) > 0$, the individual joins the union with certainty.

In other words, the degree of appeal must be positive over the last two periods for the individual to become a union member in any case.

If the individual joins the union, the probability of his actually being employed is expressed by $\Pi_t = n_t/m_t$ and the average income he hopes for may be written:

$$h_t(k) = \Pi_t \sigma_t + (1 - \Pi_t) \underline{w}(k) \tag{1}$$

---

[2] By assumption s_t is the maximum of the possible equilibrium wages.

The individual compares his hopes of income to the salary s_t available on the free market. The degree of union appeal increases if $h_t(k) > s_t$ and is lowered in the opposite case:

$$a_{t+1}(k) = a_t(k) + \mu\,[h_t(k) - s_t] \tag{2}$$

$\mu(.)$ being a strictly increasing function such that $\mu(0) = 0$.

Thus the individual does not abruptly modify his attitude with regard to the union. He adopts, on the contrary, a behaviour pattern of progressive adaptation.

Firm behaviour

In like manner, firm i is characterized throughout period t by a threshold of negotiation with the union $b_t(i)$. Contacted by the union, the firm:

- refuses union propositions if $b_t(i) < \sigma_t$;
- signs a protocol agreement if $b_t(i) > \sigma_t$.

Nevertheless, after having signed a protocol, a firm may unilaterally denounce it with a certain probability. It is accepted that, if this is so, the union, as a measure of retaliation, forbids its members to work for any firm whatever during that period. In this case, all the firms find themselves on the free market. We shall hereafter use the term betrayal to designate the situation in which a firm cancels a protocol agreement.

As for the threshold of negotiation, the firm adapts it for period $(t + 1)$ with respect to the data from period t:

- If the firm refused the union's offer, it increases $b_t(i)$ by one unit if it observes that the salary on the free market is greater than the union salary $(s_t > \sigma_t)$,[3] leaves the threshold constant if $s_0 \leq s_t \leq \sigma_t$, and lowers it—that is, hardens its position—if $s_t < s_0$.
- If the firm signed a protocol and then betrayed it, it does not modify the threshold if $s_t \geq \sigma_t$ and lowers it to just below the union salary if $s_t < \sigma_t$; in any case, the firm does not take the option of betrayal in two consecutive periods.
- If the firm respected the protocol it does not change its threshold.

Thus, like individuals, the firms adapt progressively. They try from time to time to escape the hold of the union, but then come up against the refusal of the whole set of members to work for them.

---

[3] Naturally, $b_t(i)$ cannot go beyond the ceiling $\bar{v}(i)$.

Union behaviour

The union naturally seeks to increase the salary that is demanded but it must also consider the risk of then having fewer firms which will deal with it. Hence the following rules of behaviour, depending upon whether or not there are firms having definitively contracted with the union:

- $n_t > 0$ the union raises its demand by one unit if $s_t > \sigma_t$, the union maintains its offer or increases it with a certain probability if $s_t \leq \sigma_t$;
- $n_t = 0$ the union maintains its offer if $s_t > \sigma_t$, the union lowers its demand by one unit if $s_t \leq \sigma_t$ (unless there were signers for the protocol, in which case it maintains the salary demanded).

In the instances that have just been described, the model presents several characteristics which should be noted:

- The actors do not adjust demands abruptly; they keep in mind—but in the form of an aggregate indicator—past events and adopt behaviour which depends on the history they have experienced.
- The salary on the free market tends to be lower than the salary on the organized market; a firm would always find it advantageous to betray if it were sure of not being imitated. Through isolated and successive betrayal the firms would provoke the progressive destruction of the union, the equilibrium salary so being established on the market. This phenomenon does not occur in the model because of the conjunction of the following two linkages:
  - as soon as a firm betrays, the unions refuse to work for all the firms having signed a protocol;
  - as the individuals do not immediately leave the union, the inflow of a supplementary labour demand on the free market makes the salary on that market rise abruptly and firms see that it is not in their short-term interest to betray the union.

The actors never give up trying to improve their situation. Thus, the union raises its demand with a certain probability as long as $n_t > 0$ and even if $\sigma_t \geq s_t$. In like fashion, a firm which did not betray in the foregoing period and which has signed a protocol does not hesitate to cancel it with a certain probability. This continual search carried out by the actors has important consequences on the convergence properties of the systems.

Union Perenniality

Two definitions are in order to begin with:

- in the course of any one period, the state of the system may be characterized by the triplet:

$$e_t = \{\sigma_t, M_t, N_t\} \tag{3}$$

which will be called a configuration;
- the connected union of size m and of salary σ will be the union made up of the first m individuals arranged in descending order of $\underline{w}(k)$ starting with the first individual for whom $\underline{w}(k) \leq \sigma$.

Using the hypotheses introduced up to this point, it is possible to demonstrate the following proposition.

Starting with any one initial configuration there exists a date T such that one of the properties given below is verified:

- the union dies out before T;
- for any date beyond T, the union exists and is connected; in this case, the labour-market presents three characteristics.

(i) The union wages lie within two fixed boundaries $\underline{\sigma}$ and $\bar{\sigma}$, depending on past changes in the market.

(ii) The number of firms contracting with the union lies within two values $\underline{n}$ and $\bar{n}$ depending on the history of the market.

(iii) The set of individuals may be separated into five related groups, the composition of which depends on the history of the market:

- one group, non-empty, of individuals belonging to the union in all periods;
- two groups, possibly empty, of individuals belonging to the union intermittently;
- two groups, possibly empty, of individuals never belonging to the union, one composed of individuals with very low minimal demands, the other composed of individuals having minimal demands greater than $\bar{\sigma}$.

We shall call the related group of individuals always belonging to the union the core, and the set of individuals who sometimes belong to the union the ring.

Thus the dynamics of the market end up, when the union does not die out, with a union which is composed on the one hand of a stable set of employees (the core) and, on the other, of the ever unsatisfied employees who perpetually vascillate between the union and the free market (the ring).

When *t* is sufficiently large, the union is always connected. On the other hand, the set of firms signing with the union—a set whose size fluctuates between two values $\underline{n}$ and $\bar{n}$—is not necessarily so.[4]

In spite of its imperfections the model allows us to understand how, starting with a situation in which only individuals and employers with no ties among them are brought together, a new institution can be constituted, assembling the workers and dividing the labour-market into two sub-markets: an organized market with an imposed salary and a free market on which the salary (a lower one) results from a confrontation between supply and demand.

But for a budding union to be transformed into a stable union, two conditions seem necessary:

● On the one hand, individuals and firms do not abruptly modify their attitudes towards the union: the individual who sees that belonging to the union was not favourable during the first period lowers the appeal index, but does not necessarily leave the union.[5] A signing firm which necessarily observes that the salary on the free market is less than the union salary contents itself with setting its negotiation threshold a bit under the union salary. The result is that the union cannot, as it is being developed, be instantaneously destroyed.

● On the other hand, the firms with ties to the union check out, by entering the free market, their interest in continuing to sign with the union, but this betrayal behaviour brings on a refusal to work by all of the union members; these are the reactions which protect the union, since the abrupt arrival of firms on the free market raises the wages on this market to the level of union wages and brings the firms back to an agreement with the union. The union would on the contrary be vulnerable if the firms betrayed one after another for a

---

[4] A set of firms of size n *is* connected if it includes, starting from a salary σ, the *n* first firms ranked in increasing order of $\bar{v}(i)$ from the first firm for which $\bar{v}(i) \geq \sigma$.

[5] The role of this individual behaviour is clearly brought out if we replace relation (2) by the relation: $a_{t+1}(k) = \lambda a_t(k) + \mu[h_t(k) - s_t]$ where $\lambda (0 < \lambda \leq 1)$ is a coefficient of oblivion. It is shown that, when λ is sufficiently small, the union certainly dies out in finite time.

sufficiently long period of time so that the individuals' confidence in the union would be eroded.

It should be noted:

- that the outcome of market change is not predetermined, the strength of the union and notably its size and the wages it demands being related to its history and not only to the initial conditions;
- that the model sets forth a case of imperfect self-organization since there exists a ring of individuals and firms with indefinitely unstable behaviour.

Naturally this model does not claim to account for reality in all its diversity: closed shop cases are infrequent in many countries where firms have retained freedom of choice in the personnel recruited. Firms may employ a large number of workers and negotiations often deal with the sharing of benefits between firms and workers, or the union organizations may attempt to develop in the workers a vision of the future which reinforces their attachment to unions whatever the immediate results of union action. But these observations merely reinforce interest in the analysis of the generating of unions in terms of self-organization.

Conditions for the Appearance of Institutions

At this stage, two lines of thought naturally enter into the analysis: the first concerns the pertinence of the processes in this chapter for the emergence of other economic institutions, the second brings up the question of the building of an eventual classification of the ways in which institutions appear in a market economy.

1. The model in this chapter can be developed in two directions which, moreover, are not incompatible.

First of all, nothing hinders our substituting a market of durable goods for the labour-market, the firms becoming consumers and the workers producers (farmers, for example). The budding union becomes a co-operative in a state of development and two prices are established on the market, the co-operative price and the 'free' price. The co-operative can, furthermore, handle the sale of members' products itself and guarantee each one the revenue $\Pi_t \sigma_t$ in exchange for the use of the fraction Π_t of its production capacity. At that point, a hierarchical firm is born on the market through the coalition of a group of producers.

But—whether the market be that of a durable commodity or that of a category of labour—the users can react by generating a counter-union. This observation brings up the problem of the creation of a partial bilateral monopoly within a market initially made up of independent buyers and sellers. An interesting research theme.

2. If we try to build a basic classification of the ways an institution emerges in a market economy, without claiming it to be exhaustive, we are led, at the end of this chapter, to distinguishing five classes of very different processes: the first four are illustrated in Chapters 7 to 10 and the fifth—though it has not been mentioned until now—is obvious:

● The first class corresponds to the appearance of categories of actors who individually take advantage of the existence of or the possibility of disequilibria on one or several markets; to speak of the birth of an institution in this case may seem incorrect, but this terminology is justified to the extent that the new actors belong to different categories from those initially present on the market.

● The second class includes the processes for forming the norms of beliefs, norms which, once established, may prove to be robust and condition behaviour for a long time. Here again the term institution may seem inappropriate; unless it is taken in a sense broad enough to cover all the regularities which are imposed on the market.

● The third class unites the processes in which market dynamics randomly give birth, in precise circumstances, to demands or to new resources, which in turn lead to the creation of new markets on which the demands are satisfied or the resources and the goods they have allowed to be produced are exchanged. In this case the institutions which appear are of the same nature as the initial institutions.

● The fourth class groups the co-operative processes in which, under the influence of a budding organization, a coalition of actors creates a new entity which splits the market into an organized market with high prices and a free market with low prices. These processes presume the progressive adaptation of actors' behaviour and the setting up of measures of retaliation in the case of a breach of contract.

The Market as Creator

● The fifth and last class encompasses the case in which an existing institution of higher rank (for example, the government or the Securities and Exchange Commission) imposes rules of operation on a market: two traditional examples are those of fixing a minimum wage on the labour-market or a guaranteed price on the grain market.

It is, however, possible to imagine mixed linkages involving processes which fall within several of the preceding categories. To furnish an example, we shall outline a model of labour-market regulation.

The labour-market, as described in Chapter 2, brings together individuals *m* in number who may be entrepreneurs, craftsmen, or workers. Periodically, elections are held, individuals having one vote each, and having a choice between two political parties, the right (*d*) and the left (*g*).

Before the election of period *t*, the two parties announce their programme, a programme which the electors supposedly deem credible:

● the right announces that it will not intervene on the labour-market and will therefore let the equilibrium wage s^* be established;
● the left declares it will impose a minimum wage $\underline{s}_t$.

Each individual is characterized by the amount of appeal the party on the left holds for him $a_t(k)$. If this indicator is negative or zero, the individual votes for the right, if it is positive, he votes for the left, with certainty when the indicator was already positive in the previous period, with a given probability when the indicator was negative or zero. Furthermore, the individual adapts the amount of appeal he feels for the left in keeping with the relation:

$$a_t(k) = a_{t-1}(k) + \mu[r_{gt}(k) - r_{dt}(k) - (c_{g,\,t-1} - c_{d,\,t-1})] \qquad (4)$$

in which:

● $r_{gt}(k)$ and $r_{dt}(k)$ denote respectively the revenue of the individual in case of a victory of the left or the right;
● $c_{g,\,t-1}$ and $c_{d,\,t-1}$ represent the cost to the individual of the victory of the left or the right when that victory obliges him to change states (craftsman, worker, or entrepreneur) in relation to period $(t-1)$;

- $\mu(.)$ is an increasing function of the argument such that $\mu(0) = 0$.

From period to period, the left adapts $\underline{s}_t$ taking into account notably the election results.

These few lines do not pretend to prove the coherence of this model (in which the right is completely passive), even less to analyse its dynamics, but rather to point out the emergence of an institution—the regulating of a labour-market—following the intervention of a dual process:

- a process of co-operation (the election) which gives control of a high ranking institution to one or other of two budding organizations (in this case the political parties);
- a process of the simple creation of the subordinate institution by the institution of higher rank.

Other aspects of the creation of institutions will be brought out in the last chapter of the book which considers change in the structures of competition.

11

Change in the Structure
of Competition

Since the dawning of their science, economists have never ceased to
be concerned with competition. Not only have they, in the last fifty
years, written entire libraries on the subject—whether it be on
perfect competition, oligopoly, or monopoly—but they have, during
the last decade, resuscitated the field by applying multiperiod game
theory, and notably the concept of perfect equilibrium (Fudenberg
and Tirole 1986), to oligopolistic situations. Progressively the gap
between the reality experienced by the head of a firm and the micro-
economist's discourse—highly useful after all—has been reduced.
But reduction does not mean disappearance.

The head of a firm concentrates above all on bringing about a
change in competition structures—by modifying his portfolio of
activities, giving up assets, making takeover bids, launching new
lines of products, controlling protected markets—in order to ensure
rents as permanent as possible. The micro-economist takes as given
the set of firms—real and potential—and poses questions on their
policies of investment, prices, quantity, and quality . . . He reasons
essentially within self-imposed competition structures.

These structures are only very partially determined by the technical
and commercial characteristics of each branch. They result largely
from historic change in the branch from the time of its origin.
Nothing demonstrates this better than the comparison of the systems
of production, transportation, and distribution of electricity in large
industrial countries. The diversity of these organizations, historically
generated by the actors' interaction, and the distribution of rents
among them, is quite surprising.

The title of this chapter therefore touches on a pertinent problem. It
does not, however, answer a twofold question: what is a structure?

How does an endogenous change in structure relate to the emergence of an institution?

1. The definition of a structure of competition presumes first of all on taking two lists as given: a list of activities and a list of strategically independent industrial groups, every group that practices an activity on the first list figuring on the second and every activity of a group on the second list figuring on the first. The definition then implies approximate knowledge in volume of the distribution of each activity among the groups on the market and of the turnover of each group among the activities. But these elements, as every strategy counsellor knows, are not sufficient for describing the limits which result concerning the possibilities for interaction among firms. Therefore, the notion of a competition structure can only take on a precise meaning within the framework of particular models.

2. Nevertheless, it is easy to understand why such structures can be assimilated to institutions: even if firms work in the long term at making them evolve, they engender rules which in the short term the firms themselves must observe.

Considering the immensity of the subject, this chapter will be limited to situating models of endogenous change in competition structures in relation to the problematics of this book. A first part will attempt to enumerate the elements to be taken into account in the building of such models, while the second part will present a few specific models.

Ingredients for Model-Building

In models of change in competition structures, the essential actor—the equivalent of the molecule in statistical thermodynamics—is obviously the firm, the centre of decision-making and resources. Therefore, at each period, the number and characteristics of these firms make up both a heritage of past history and a limiting framework for future possibilities.

Within this framework, the firms put goods or services—perfect or imperfect substitutes for each other—on the market and find themselves faced with a demand which may:

- either be as described in Chapter 5 with individualization of buyers and uncertainty as to the volume demanded of each firm;

- or globalized, the market having the time to reach equilibrium in each period.

But here an important dichotomy between two families of models enters in: the downstream models which exclude purchases (or mergers) between firms and are concerned only with the downstream market for the firms' products, and the upstream–downstream models which presume the existence of another market, an upstream capital market on which the goods exchanged are shares in the firms and the actors are the firms themselves.

Let us begin with the ingredients for the downstream models. It seems to me that they belong to four categories:

1. Defining these models first assumes that the conditions for the birth or death of a firm be determined.

In the role of Thanatos, the model-builder has a choice between two possible options:

- to have the firm disappear when its average profitability has proven insufficient over the last few periods;
- to eliminate the firm as soon as its cash flow becomes negative.

The advantage of this second option is explicitly to bring in balance-sheet constraints—very important in reality—by introducing, as a heritage of the past, the volume of financial resources which the firm's executives have at their disposal.

As the creator, the model-builder has even greater freedom. He can set the number of entries authorized per period, the cost of entry in relation to market conditions, the capacity allowed a new firm, the means of determining the production costs of that firm, the data which determine the anticipations of profit based on which a potential firm becomes a reality or not, and so on.

2. In a second stage, the variables which firms can act upon and the rules of decision—of bounded rationality—attributed to these firms should be enumerated. Through these choices, the model-builder reveals the vision of reality he is trying to represent. Among the variables which, for one reason or another, deserve to be included are:

- the range of qualities offered;
- the prices and/or the quantities of the different products proposed as in Chapter 5;
- the volume of capacity or productivity investment;

- the intensity of research and development outlay (or better, of innovation outlay);
- the intensity of imitation efforts (to adopt innovations from without);
- the volume of technology sales or purchases (to gain access to innovations of other firms).

For each of these variables, the rules of decision may vary fairly largely. A single example is enough to demonstrate this: for the intensity of innovation outlay, three hypotheses are conceivable, a constant outlay (which may differ among the firms), an outlay which increases when the firm's finances improve (advantage is taken of the abundance of available resources), an outlay which increases, on the contrary, when the firm's situation worsens (a firm tries to innovate out of necessity when the vice of competition tightens).

The choice of variables and the rules of decision create a dichotomy within the downstream models by separating the homogeneous models in which the behaviour of all the firms falls in the same class, from the heterogeneous models (Chiappori 1984, Conlisk 1989) which introduce two or more groups of firms each having distinct behaviour.

3. The third category of ingredients is a mixture of more varied elements. One must indeed describe:

- the information—incomplete or imperfect—which the firms dispose of for decision-making;
- the random processes which determine the results of innovation outlay;
- the random processes of diffusion which give firms a certain knowledge of other firms' innovations so they can imitate their technology or try to acquire it;
- the relations which determine the operating costs of a company in relation to economies of scale, the volume of cumulated production, the amount of productivity investment, and the influence of innovations and imitation efforts.

4. Lastly, one must not forget to determine the devolution of profits in case a role is planned for the supply of financial resources available. It is in fact indispensable to calculate these resources since their volume limits the firm's investment possibilities. It is useful, besides, to check along the way to see that the model does

not authorize an indefinite accumulation of funds by the firms, an eventuality which would clearly be unrealistic.

Let us now deal with upstream–downstream models. What supplementary ingredients does their construction assume? It seems to me convenient to divide them into three groups.

1. The upstream market is open in all periods. In the course of a period any firm which is not acquired itself may acquire another one and only one. When firm i has acquired firm j in period t, these two firms are considered a single entity at period $(t + 1)$.

2. It is therefore necessary to be able to describe the characteristics of the new firm based on those of its two components. If the production capacities seem additive a priori, the model-builder must choose as to technologies: will alignment be made on the best technology or on that of the firm taking over and what will be the cost of making the production apparatus uniform?[1]

3. A third stage consists of defining how each firm i determines the maximum value it attributes to firm j in period t, $\bar{v}_t(i, j)$ (for $i \neq j$) and the minimum value which its stockholders attribute to the company itself $\bar{v}_t(i, i)$; knowledge of these values makes it possible to specify the interval, eventually empty, of possible purchase prices i would pay for j: $[\bar{v}_t(j, j), \bar{v}_t(i, j)]$.

Estimating $\bar{v}_t(i, i)$ is a delicate task since the future of firm i is quite uncertain: it may remain independent, ultimately acquire other firms, or be taken over itself in the course of following periods . . . One rule, which is close to the financial analysts' practices, might be to multiply the last known profit $b_{i, t-1}$, by a coefficient K^i_t and to add to this product the sum f_{it} of available funds:

$$\bar{v}_t(i, i) = f_{it} + K^i_t b_{i, t-1} \tag{1}$$

As for the coefficient K^i_t, it would be adjusted, up or down, from period to period according to the increase or decrease in profits.

Still more difficult is the evaluation of $\bar{v}_t(i, j)$. If it is accepted that the situation of all the firms is common knowledge, we might assume a two-step evaluation:

---

[1] This question may be surprising, but observation has shown that in certain cases the firm taking over may prove incapable of assimilating the technology of the firm bought out (following, for instance, the departure of the most competent staff members).

● In the first step, firm i evaluates the profits of period $(t + 1)$ with and without the takeover and calculates:

$$\bar{v}'_t(i,j) = f_{jt} + \delta k^{ij}_t [b_{(i+j), t+1}] \tag{2}$$

$\delta(0 < \delta < 1)$ being a discount coefficient over one period and K^{ij}_t the multiplier that firm i accords to the additional profits generated by the takeover in period $(t + 1)$ (if firm i has confidence in its management capacity, an admissible hypothesis would be for it to assume $K^{ij}_t = K^i_t$).

● In the second step, company i estimates the fraction $\alpha(0 < \alpha < 1)$ of its reserves that it can devote to the acquisition of j and retains for the maximum purchase price, the value:

$$\bar{v}_t(i,j) = \min [\alpha f_{it}, \bar{v}'_t(i,j)] \tag{3}$$

The coefficient α must naturally depend on the abundance of firm i's funds in relation to the volume of its activities.

4. There remains the possible operating of the upstream market to be described. Is this a conceivable mechanism? Here is one illustration among others. The firms enter the market one after the other in random order as eventual takeover firms.

Let us assume that the first be firm i_0. It considers the sub-set $J(i_0)$ of firms j for which it could make an admissible offer—that is, such that:

$$\bar{v}_t(i_0, j) \geq \bar{v}_t (j, j) \tag{4}$$

It then chooses out of $J(i_0)$ the firm or one of the firms having the maximum value $\bar{v}'_t(i_0, j)$. Let j_0 be that firm: the firm i_0 proposes a price $p(i_0, j_0)$ within the admissible range. From that point on, during that period:

● no purchase offer can any longer be made for firm i_0;
● the firm j_0 can no longer operate as an eventual takeover firm.

Then the firm i_1 comes along and the process repeats itself with only one modification: firm i_1 must adopt $p(i_0, j_0)$ as the minimum value of j_0.

When all the firms have appeared on the market, the firms which have been the object of a purchase proposition are assumed to be acquired by the bidder who made the highest offer.

These few lines merely pretend to outline the possible paths for model-building. They do, however, bring out, in comparison with the four preceding chapters, two new modalities for the emergence of an institution:

● An institution may be transformed because its operation modifies the number and size of the actors and as a consequence the nature of the relations which the surviving actors must take into account (the elementary example is that of a duopoly transformed into a monopoly through the bankruptcy of one of the two firms in the duopoly).

● An institution may generate a new one because the actors operating within it can simultaneously intervene on a 'metalevel', some taking control of others and so modifying their size and number.

The first of these two modalities will now be illustrated in a few specific models.

A Few Models of Change in Competition Structures

Three models will help us bring out several aspects of change in competition structures.

A simple model of natural selection

The first of these models, proposed by Chiappori in 1984, aims at analysing the influence of competition—as a mechanism of natural selection—on the composition of the population of the firms present on the market. It postulates the existence of two types of firm, optimizing (O) and sub-optimizing (S), each firm being characterized, at a given moment, by its size—supposedly whole—q.

The optimizing firms develop and have, from period t to period $(t + 1)$ the probability p of seeing their size increase by a unit. They may also degenerate with probability π by becoming a sub-optimizing firm, size being constant. Consequently, they have the probability $(1 - p - \pi)$ of remaining in an unchanged state.

For their part, the sub-optimizing firms tend to regress and have, from period t to period $(t + 1)$, the probability p' of seeing their size diminish by a unit. They may also improve, size being constant, and adopt, with probability π', the behaviour of an optimizing firm. Their state thus remains unchanged with the probability $(1 - p' - \pi')$.

In addition there exists a maximum firm size $(Q+1)$. Once it has reached this size, a firm can only maintain itself or decline.

Two dynamics are then examined.

1. The first assumes the existence of an environment E made up of 'potential' firms. The probability of the transformation, during period t, of a potential firm into a size 1 firm—necessarily optimizing—is designated by r while a size 1 sub-optimizing firm has the probability p' of becoming potential.

We are naturally concerned with the distribution, by size and type of firm population, when time increases indefinitely—that is, with numbers O_q, s_q, e which represent respectively, in a stationary state, the fraction of size q optimizing firms, of size q sub-optimising firms, and of potential firms. When the entries and exits balance out for sufficiently large t ($re = p's_1$), the calculation shows that the form of this distribution depends on the coefficient:

$$\lambda = [p\Pi' + p'] / [p'(\Pi + p)] \tag{5}$$

● If $\lambda < 1$, we obtain a decreasing exponential distribution in which the number of firms of a given size diminishes with size. A situation all the more probable as π and p' are large (high risk of decline, rapid disappearance of sub-optimizing firms) and p and π' are small (slow growth of optimizing firms, low proportion of firms improving their performance from one period to another).

● If $\lambda > 1$, the distribution is exponentially increasing: the most numerous firms are the large-sized ones.

As for the ratio ρ of the total number of sub-optimizing firms to the total number of optimizing firms, it is strictly positive whenever $\pi > 0$; in other words, the possibility of the degeneration of an optimizing firm's management is sufficient to maintain sub-optimizing firms in the observed population indefinitely.

2. The second dynamic adds the existence of two potential states O_0 and S_0, characterizing respectively potential optimizing and sub-optimizing entrepreneurs, and accepts the possibility of the entry of new entrepreneurs in all states.

The calculation then shows that, when the number of entries is proportional to the total number of firms in the economy, the ratio of the total number of sub-optimizing firms to the total number of optimizing firms tends to a number ρ:

$$\rho = [\pi + K_s] / [\pi' + K_0] \tag{6}$$

K_s and K_0 being coefficients characterizing the optimizing and sub-optimizing firms' rate of entry.

We therefore have, for high t, a strictly positive proportion of sub-optimizing firms. This proportion increases, in a natural fashion, with the probability of degeneration and the total influx of sub-optimizing firms. It is a decreasing function of the probability of improvement and of the total influx of optimizing firms. On the other hand, it is independent of probabilities p and p', that is of the firms' growth–disappearance mechanism. (Chiappori 1984: 101)

Resituated within the perspectives of this book, four points follow from the Chiappori model:

(i) Instead of being considered as exogenous data, the probabilities p, p', π and π' could be related to the firms' internal decision-making process:

- an optimizing firm makes benefits which allow it to increase its capacity and attempt to increase its share of the market; a sub-optimizing firm may on the other hand, for lack of financial resources, have trouble renewing its production capacity and maintaining its sales volume;
- being profitable, an optimizing firm is always threatened with 'numbness' and ossification, while in the sub-optimizing firm the worsening of results often provokes crises which engender changes in management and policy modifications.

(ii) In the first dynamic, the economy moves towards a stationary equilibrium in which the distribution of firm population according to size and type is steady, but at the firm level evolution continues and will never come to an end. In other words, the stationary equilibrium can only be established thanks to the permanent entry of optimizing firms on to the market.

If, on the contrary, we exclude the appearance of new firms, all the initial firms have a non-zero probability of dying out but the life expectancy is naturally longer for the optimizing firms than for the sub-optimizing ones. Under the assumption that, at horizon T, a discontinuity intervenes in market conditions, a discontinuity which cancels out the probabilities p, p', π and π' and blocks firm evolution, the economy may at that time find itself in a multitude of stable states which differ in the number, size, and type of existing firms. This assumption may seem artificial, but it has the merit of revealing affinities which exist between the Chiappori model and the path dependent equilibrium models in this book. Is this assumption really so arbitrary then? It is not so sure, since in reality the probabilities p, p', π, π' are never constant over a long period: the market for a commodity may stagnate and stockholders of optimizing firms decide to distribute the total amount of profits, which would annul p and at the same time allow the sub-optimizing firms to maintain themselves with no loss of markets ($p'=0$) and without internal crises ending up in an improvement in their management ($\pi' = 0$); lastly, technology in the sector may cease to evolve, which reduces the risk of the optimizing firms' degenerating ($\pi = 0$).

Thus the models with stationary equilibria and models with path dependent stable states appear in many ways to be close and complementary visions of reality.

(iii) Whether one adopts one of these visions or the other, it must be stressed that, for those acquiring a commodity produced in the sector, the competition structure—and therefore the price conditions—differ at every finite date T, in relation to its history. Hence an irreversible influence of the structure of the sector on the possibilities for development of the rest of the economy.

(iv) There is nevertheless one aspect that the Chiappori model does not illustrate and that is the influence of the structure of competition on firm behaviour. Indeed, the probabilities p, p', π, π' are supposedly fixed and not modified in relation to conditions reigning on the downstream market, conditions determined, at least in part, by the number, size, and type of existing firms. Consequently, in its original form, the Chiappori model does not really have competition structure play the role of an institution.

A model of the evolution of competition towards a monopoly or an oligopoly

The second model presented, that of Laslier (1989) is, in many respects, less satisfying than the preceding one, but it has the advantage of linking better the state of the market to firm behaviour.

In this model, the companies in competition are indefinite in number, no entry taking place on to the market. The total benefits of any one firm, firm i, take the form:

$$B(i) = N(i)b(i) \tag{7}$$

where $N(i)$ is the number of units and $b(i)$ the benefit per unit. By using available funds which result from past operations, firm i can invest, either to increase its production capacity, which would allow it to increase $N(i)$, or to improve its productivity which would allow it to increase $b(i)$.

But the firms are in competition with each other for a share of a set amount of stock of a resource which may either be a production factor (total available volume of highly qualified labour or the production of a raw material), or a quantity sold (total volume of the contracts consumers are willing to sign). In the description of the model it will be assumed that the stock concerns the number of qualified workers available. The other presentations of the apologue would take but marginal modifications.

In terms of the chosen plot, the hypotheses of the model concern the workers, the firms, the market dynamics, the entrepreneurs' behaviour, the encounters between firms and workers, and the policy of recruitment.

1. The qualified workers are identical, ready to work for any one of the firms, at any wage, willing to change employment as soon as they get a higher wage offer. The labour-market operates in such a way that all workers are employed in every period.

2. At date t, every firm i is characterized by six parameters: (i) its staff $N_t(i)$; (ii) its labour productivity expressed in value $v_t(i)$ (it is assumed that the firm has a linear production function, using only the labour factor, the value of firm $i's$ production for period t being $(v_t(i)\ N_t(i))$; (iii) its capacity $K_t(i)$ which limits its staff ($N_t(i) \le K_t(i)$); (iv) its wage level $s_t(i)$ which, along with the preceding parameters, defines the benefits $B_t(i) = N_t(i)\ [v_t(i) - s_t(i)]$ of the firm (the wage varies from one firm to another, but the employees of a given firm all receive the same wages for period t); (v) the accumulated savings of the firm $E_t(i)$ which serve to finance investments; (vi) the firm's propensity for savings $a(i)$ which denotes the fraction of the benefits immediately saved by the firm.

Four other parameters are common to all the firms:

- the gain in productivity P; a firm that invests in productivity sees it increase from $v_t(i)$ to $v_{t+1}(i) = v_t(i) + P$;
- the cost of investment in productivity c_p which must be taken out of the accumulated savings at the time of investment;
- the cost of investment in capacity c_c which allows the firm to increase in size by a unit: $K_{t+1}(i) = K_t(i) + 1$;
- the coefficient multiplier of savings: θ.

The introduction of this last coefficient deserves some comment. Laslier assumes that the firm's available accumulated savings at the beginning of period $(t + 1)$ are expressed by:

$$E_{t+1}(i) = \theta E_t(i) + a(i)B_t(i) - I_t(i) \qquad (8)$$

in which $I_t(i)$ represents the investments of period t in capacity or in productivity. In relation (8), the coefficient θ may be given various interpretations:

$\theta \geq 1$: the firm places its accumulated savings at an interest rate which is positive or zero and can dispose of them at any time.

$\theta < 1$: the firm sees its available accumulated savings dwindle as a consequence of poor placements in other activities leading to the depreciation of assets, either out of the obligation it is under to put a part of those savings, in various forms, at the disposal of stockholders (the case of a subsidiary largely controlled by a majority stockholder), or out of the necessity of freezing a part of those savings in order to meet unforeseen circumstances.

3. From a dynamics point of view, each period may be considered to be divided up into three successive sub-periods:

- a sub-period of production at the end of which every firm knows its benefits $B_t(i)$;
- a sub-period of investment during which the firm chooses according to its self-financing capacity $\theta E_t(i) + a(i) B_t(i)$, to invest in capacity, invest in productivity, or not to invest;
- a sub-period of recruitment during which a random contact is made between firm i and worker k with the possibility of the worker's being recruited at salary $s_t(i)$ if $s_t(i) > s_t(k)$, or if $s_t(i) \leq s_t(k)$, at salary $s_t(i) + 1$.

Thus the only random element is the chance drawing of the firm and the worker that will enter into contact. It should be noted that, in all periods, all firms produce and can invest but only one of them can recruit (and then only one worker).

4. Firm behaviour is described with simple but plausible rules:

- a firm which is not at full capacity does not seek to increase this capacity; so if it can invest, it does so in productivity;
- a firm at full capacity always considers that, if it increases its capacity, to recruit an additional worker it will have to increase wages by a unit; to determine its decision it will therefore calculate the following benefits:

$$\begin{cases} BC = [N_t(i) + 1][v_t(i) - s_t(i) - 1] \\ BP = N_t(i)[v_t(i) + P - s_t(i)] \end{cases} \tag{9}$$

- the firm does not consider the investment costs c_p and c_c; the existence of these costs keeps the firms from investing continually but does not lead to substitution between the two forms of investment; this hypothesis which may seem excessive is justified by the definitive character in the model of gains in productivity and increases in capacity.

From these three rules, comes the following firm behaviour ($E'_t(i)$ designating the capacity of self-financement $\theta E_t(i) + a(i)$ $B_t(i)$ of firm i):

- if $N_t(i) < K_t(i)$ and $E'_t(i) \geq c_p$, the firm invests in productivity;
- if $N_t(i) = K_t(i)$ and $BC < BP$, $E'_t(i) \geq c_p$, the firm invests in productivity;
- if $N_t(i) = K_t(i)$ and $BC \leq BP$, $E'_t(i) \geq c_c$, the firm invests in capacity.

In the other cases, the firm does not invest.

Naturally, if the firm invests in capacity (and respectively in productivity), its savings are lowered by c_c (and respectively by c_p).

5. A firm is said to be alive if it employs at least one worker; otherwise it is dead—as Monsieur de la Palisse would have said—and that death is definitive. The random encounter between a firm and a worker not part of its personnel is the result of the chance drawing of a couple of living firms, the first firm in the couple being that which will perhaps recruit, and the second that which will perhaps lose a worker. Every encounter has a non-zero probability of occurring.

6. Firm i will recruit a worker from j on the condition that its capacity permits it and that the salary it offers is of interest. We must therefore assume $N_t(i) < K_t(i)$. Under these circumstances:

- if $s_t(j) < s_t(i)$, the firm recruits the worker at wage $s_t(i)$;
- if $s_t(j) \geq s_t(i)$, firm i plans on proposing wage $s_t(i) + 1$, but it must then increase the wages of all its workers; consequently it compares its current benefits $N_t(i)[v_{t+1}(i) - s_t(i)]$ to the benefits in the case of recruitment $[N_t(i) + 1][v_{t+1}(i) - s_t(i) - 1]$ and chooses the most economic solution.

What changes are generated by the dynamics of this model?

If $\theta \geq 1$, the process converges in probability, whatever the initial data given, to a state in which all workers are employed by a single company in a monopolistic situation, but the winning firm cannot be designated in advance as every living firm *i* in any one period has a non-zero probability of becoming monopolistic.

If $\theta < 1$, none of the preceding general results remains true. Simulations show that depending on the initial data given, several types of trajectory are possible. For example, by simulating change in the competition structure starting with an initial situation of four firms employing five workers each and having respective initial productivities of 30, 31, 32, and 33, Laslier brought out in examples (for $a(i) = 1$ and $P = 1$) multiple dynamic configurations:

(i) The simulations all end up in a monopoly, the monopolist may be any one of the initial firms (for this example $\theta = 0.84$, $c_p = 400$, $c_c = 250$, the initial wages being at 18).

(ii) The simulations end up in varied trajectories (for this example $\theta = 0.62$, $c_p = 185$, $c_c = 150$, the initial wages being at 20):

- a firm conquers the whole market and finds itself in a monopoly position;
- only two or three firms remain in the final state;
- all four firms remain alive (thus, in certain simulations the workers were exchanged among the firms which caused a rise in wages, but no firm invested in productivity and the benefits dwindled to the point of keeping the firms from accumulating enough savings to invest).

An improvement in the rules of conduct followed by certain firms would increase their probability of survival, but it would probably not reduce the range of possible outcomes.

Three final remarks allow us to evaluate better the importance of this model:

- As opposed to the Chiappori model, the model by Laslier is uniform since the same rules define the behaviour of all firms. They are common-sense rules, but their application by a firm may prove unfortunate in certain circumstances. In other words, we sometimes observe afterwards that the behaviour of such and such a firm at a given date has proven to be a mistake considering the future evolution of the environment.

- The model establishes an explicit link between the firm's past choices, its current market situation, and the margin for manœuvre that it has; in this respect, it introduces, but in a summary manner, the reaction loop which links firms to each other. However, the firms do not in this model show strategic behaviour: they do not, when they become few in number, anticipate the behaviour of their competitors in order to deduce from it the policy they should follow.

● It is interesting to note that, according to the values of the parameters, the outcome of change in competition structures is either foreseeable or not. Now, the final state of the structure of competition is essential for the rest of the economy (represented by the workers or the buyers of the product) since the wage levels or the sales prices,[2] in the final stage of the simulations, largely depend on the trajectory followed.

A model on innovation and technological imitation

The third model which will be outlined—the richest of the three—was proposed by Nelson and Winters (1982). This model is built upon five principal hypotheses.

1. It considers an industry initially composed of N firms producing the same good or service. For period t, the production of q_{it} of firm i is proportional to the production capacity K_{it} of that firm:

$$q_{it} = a_{it} K_{it} \qquad (10)$$

The coefficient a_{it} of capital productivity in this model completely summarizes the characteristics of the technology employed by firm i at period t.

2. The total production of the industry q_t being the sum of the firms' production, the product market rapidly converges to a stable state in which the price p_t generates a level of demand equal to the offer:

$$q_t = \sum_i q_{it} \qquad (11)$$

$$p_t = d(q_t) \qquad (12)$$

3. The profit of firm i per unit of production capacity is expressed by:

$$\Pi_{it} = p_t a_{it} - c - r_{imt} - r_{int} \qquad (13)$$

c designating the production cost per unit of capacity while r_{imt} and r_{int} are the respective amounts of the research and development

---

[2] When the quantity set concerns the volume of contracts signed by the buyers.

costs which the firm devotes to imitation and innovation per unit of capital.

4. The firm's activity in R. & D. generates progress in productivity as a result of a two-stage random process:

- During the first stage, the firm draws at random two variables d_{imt} and d_{int}. The first of these variables corresponds to the possibility of improving productivity through imitation. It may take on two values 0 and 1. When $d_{imt} = 0$, the firm's R. & D. outlay in view of imitating existing technologies fails. When $d_{imt} = 1$, the firm is in a position to implement the best known technology.

The second variable corresponds to the other path of technical progress, innovation. It can also take on the values 0 and 1. When $d_{int} = 0$, the firm discovers no new technology. When $d_{int} = 1$, it discovers a new technology but one which can be uninteresting. The probabilities of success of firm i's R. & D. outlay are supposedly proportional to R. & D. expenditures.

$$\text{prob}\,[d_{imt} = 1] = \min\,[a_m\, r_{imt}\, K_{it},\, 1] \tag{14}$$

$$\text{prob}\,[d_{int} = 1] = \min\,[a_n\, r_{int}\, K_{it},\, 1] \tag{15}$$

a_m and a_n being constant coefficients representing in a way the productivities of the two forms of R. & D. expenditures.

- The second stage comes into being only in the case of the firm's success with at least one of the R. & D. outlays.

If $d_{int} = 1$, the firm has random access to a new technology drawn from a set of potential technologies $F[A, t, a_{it}]$ which depends on the set of conceivable technologies A of period t and on the firm's current technology. For this new technology the capital productivity is $\bar{a}_{it}$.

If $d_{imt} = 1$, the firm, as stated earlier, has certain access to the best technology in use $\hat{a}_t$.

Consequently, in case of a double discovery, the technology of firm i at period $(t + 1)$ becomes:

$$a_{i,\,t+1} = \max\,[a_{it},\, \hat{a}_t\, \bar{a}_{it}] \tag{16}$$

5. Finally, the firm's production capacity at period $(t + 1)$ is defined by a relation of the form:

$$K_{i,\,t+1} = I[\,p_t\, a_{it}\,/\,c,\, q_{it},\, \Pi_{it}\,] + (1 - \delta)K_{it} \tag{17}$$

δ being a coefficient of depreciation and I a non-negative investment function whose arguments are the profit margin $p_t q_{it}/c$, the production and profit per unit of capacity. This function is supposedly non-decreasing in its first argument, non-increasing in the others. The authors legitimately accept that investment is null when the profit margin is equal to 1, the market share negligible, and profits null.

What do we learn about the structures of competition from such a model?

1. If the firms make no R. & D. outlay ($r_{imt} = r_{int} = 0$ for every i and every t), and all have the same capital productivity ($a_{it} = a$), the model dynamics become deterministic. The firms are distinguished only by their initial capacity K_{io} (and the resulting production q_{io}). There exist then, in the absence of entries, equilibria in which the N firms share the market equally. The entry of new firms having the same productivity has no major effect on the nature of the final competitive structure.

2. Even in the absence of R. & D. spending, the situation is more complex when the firms differ in capital productivity. In the absence of entries, the N initial firms can survive but with unequal shares of the market if the differences in productivity remain low: when they become substantial, the N_1 firms having the highest productivity can eliminate the others and divide the market up equally.

3. If innovation spending is null ($r_{int} = 0$ for every i and every t) but imitation expenditures positive and identical for all the firms, the surviving companies will all have in finite time a capital productivity equal to the maximum productivity observed in the initial state; as for the number of surviving firms, it will depend on the assumptions made on the declining firms leaving the market. The random nature of the imitiation process will generally engender the appearance of a plurality of stable states.

Thus, in the absence of 'fundamental' technical progress, firm behaviour in matters of imitation (that is, the choice of r_{imt}'s) and the means of diffusing knowledge will influence the competition structure which will be established in the end.

4. If innovation and imitation spending are both positive, at least for certain firms, the paths become much more complicated and depend on the numerical data chosen to define the model—that is:

- the number, size, and level of productivity of firms existing in the initial state;
- the elasticity of product demand in that branch;

- the financial constraints limiting the firms' investment possibilities;
- the probabilities for success in the two forms of research and development;
- the evolution, in relation to time, of the levels of productivity in the new technologies likely to be discovered;
- firms' behaviour in R. & D. and, when this is constant in time, the initial characteristics of the firms in the four categories: innovative and imitative, innovative, imitative, and passive.

On a methodological level, this model perfectly illustrates three aspects of the work on the evolution of structures of competition:

- it underscores the importance of conditions for the incoming and outgoing of firms on the market;
- it shows that, if the technological boundary is time dependent, the search for stable states is replaced by the study of paths;
- it confirms that, if the processes are complex, the general theorems are difficult to obtain and the use of simulations becomes inevitable.

But what does this model teach us about self-organization phenomena? It leads, as I see it, to four lines of thought.

1. It brings out, along the lines of work by Schumpeter and numerous other economists, the creative role for self-organization of the agents' research in technological innovation. By simultaneously introducing imitation research, it proposes, in addition, a dichotomy in research behaviour, which in view of the analyses in this book, might have broader significance. It seems indeed useful to distinguish between:

- on the one hand, the research behaviour giving access to information already held by other agents (this is the behaviour which constantly appears in the first part of the book);
- on the other hand, the research behaviour allowing the discovery of information at least temporarily exclusive; this second category appeared for the first time in Chapter 7 when the birth of a recruitment agency implied that an individual possessed a specific information technology.

These two categories of research behaviour naturally have opposite effects on the relative situations of individuals since the first tends to make these situations uniform by spreading information while the second introduces differences by generating particular knowledge.

2. By introducing the concepts of innovation and imitation, the model implicitly raises the question of how a firm goes about perfecting a technology. In reality, the discovery of a new technology often means mastering a set of elementary technologies some of which come from other sectors through diffusion processes, some of which are borrowed from competitors, and some others of which result from specific innovations. Hence, after a long maturing process, the possibility of ruptures when all of the conditions are united. The study of such phenomena is clearly of primary importance for understanding the relations between self-organization and technical progress.

3. Though it does have the advantage of detailing the processes of innovation and imitation, the Nelson and Winters model, on the other hand, has the disadvantage of not describing the rules the firms use for setting the level of R. & D. These rules, however, are important for two reasons:

• They express the firm's response to market signals (price and quantity) and allow the change in competition structures to be made endogenous.
• They express the specific nature of decision-making within each firm, a specificity which should not be overlooked: already, in Chapter 5, the properties of the stable states depended on the existence of retailers having particular behaviour patterns; such a result should be confirmed through the study of change in the structures of competition. How can one in fact not foresee that the final stage of an oligopoly will be highly different according to the strategies of the firms that form it, this stage depending, for example, on whether all the firms only proceed with research under pressure of necessity or whether one of them constantly destabilizes its rivals through incessant innovations?

This remark on the influence of the specific nature of rules proper to each agent naturally leads on to considering questions—which we shall do in the Epilogue—on that old issue of the impact of personalities and exceptional teams on the future of evolution.

4. The dynamics of the Nelson and Winters model result in a more or less sizeable and rapid random decrease in the equilibrium market price for the product offered by the industry. Hence the possibility of considerable repercussions on the rest of the economy,

since the firms using the product as a factor may either become quickly profitable, begin a take-off, and grow by taking advantage of their own economies of scale, or be forced to put off their entry on the market for lack of suppliers at a satisfactory cost and thereafter come up against obstacles resulting from the scale at which competitors are operating. Therefore, this type of model-building, more naturally than traditional micro-economic theory, ends up with phenomena of decline or cumulative development.

Certainly, economic literature is not restricted to the three foregoing models, but the latter have merit in illustrating a few essential linkages and in stimulating a redoubling of research efforts in this field.

Suggestions for Eventual Research

Three roads are certainly worth exploring.

A first suggestion flows directly from analysis of the models: an effort must clearly be made to formulate the rules of limited rationality which describe firm behaviour and to examine the consequences for the dynamics of competition structures of a homogeneity or heterogeneity in the behaviour of firms composing the industry.

The second suggestion, for its part, has not yet been mentioned in this chapter. Here it is summed up in a few lines: economic theory introduces a deep rift between perfect competition and oligopolistic situations; on one side, firms consider the price imposed, on the other, they seek to modify their environment and even to anticipate the reactions of competitors. But, the moment a cross-over must be accounted for without rupture in the agents' behaviour, from perfect (or nearly perfect) competition to an oligopolistic situation, it is necessary for firms to show from the start, through their rules of conduct, their desire to influence market conditions and their ability to take into account the decision of others and for competition structures progressively to cease to annihilate these dimensions in firm behaviour. The same mechanisms must naturally work the other way when the continuous entry of firms on to the market disaggregates an oligopoly and transforms it into nearly perfect competition.

Last of all, there is a third suggestion: an attempt should be made at building models in which the firms' managements act on competitive structures on two levels: on the one hand by offering, on the downstream market, products whose nature and price make it impossible for competitors to maintain their activity, on the other hand by acquiring, on the upstream market, assets which cease to have independent management. Recourse to these two types of decision presumes deliberation in the use of the resources the firms have at their disposal.

There is still a long way to go, therefore, before the elaboration of a satisfactory theory on endogenous change in competition structures, but the outlines of such a theory are beginning to appear, and these already allow a deeper understanding of the factors which, through the intermediary of self-organization processes, generate institutional structures which are favourable or unfavourable to development.

The analysis of the change in competitive structures will be at the heart of our third volume, when we will take into account material from the second volume about firms' internal self-organization processes. From that point of view, the present chapter is only an introduction.

Epilogue

This book could end with a line of omission points or question marks. Points of omission because, in spite of the underlying effort to be coherent, it has made but sparse clearings on the edge of an immense forest and can only conclude with an invitation for further research. Question marks because it appeals to concepts with outlines as yet poorly defined and explores a theoretical approach whose contribution to the science of economics cannot as yet be said to be either marginal or essential.

Thus these last few pages deserve the title of epilogue rather than conclusion. A mixture of remarks, questions, reflections, and propositions, they attempt to clarify certain developments in the book and to discern themes for future research. They touch on a variety of subjects, from the destructive properties of markets to the concept of self-organization, from problems of modelling to the means of handling time, from the role of limited rationality behaviour to the introduction of chance, from the influence of exceptional figures to the link between the dynamics of markets and that of hierarchies.

The Destructive Market

As is reflected in the title of the book, the market is not only an organizer and a creator, it is also a destroyer. There is nothing new in this remark: economists announced it long ago. More recently, systemics has taught us that the creation of order feeds on disorder and that destruction accompanies creation. Several chapters of the book, therefore, help us to understand how the market operates from this point of view.

1. Once again, I shall start with the simple model given in Chapter 3. Every outside shock which modifies the ceilings and bottom limits

of actors' demands destroys the stable states, gears the workers' search for jobs to negotiations, and sets off new dynamics. Disorder follows order and may prepare for a new order, destroying agents along the way. But if the latter have no choice but to perish or adapt, it is because the price results from an anonymous process of self-organization. If markets operated with auctioneers in Walras fashion, the workers in firms on the decline would know who to threaten or hang in effigy. Who can they turn on when each firm or each employee is limited to reacting to the local environment? Daily observations confirm this analysis: while governments, whatever the weight of budget constraints, sweat blood and tears to close down even the smallest administration or reduce the staff of a state monopoly, the market from year to year silently crushes multitudes of firms and forces thousands of workers to be recycled. A phenomenon which supply and demand curves do not explain but which the endogenous dynamics in Chapter 3 help us to understand.

2. Several chapters mentioned the possibility of markets without stable states being in permanent random disorder as a result of the rigidity of agents' demands (Chapter 3), of the limited nature of their rationality (Chapter 5), of their inability to infer quality (Chapter 6), or because of their potential for disturbing equilibria (Chapter 7). It thus appears that the aptitude of the market for self-organization is not only partial, as shown in Chapter 4, but may, in certain circumstances, be shown to be faulty. One can therefore say, with some abuse of language, that independently of the effects mentioned in the previous paragraph, market processes are likely to have destructive influences in a dual manner:

- by trapping the agents in stable states, thus rendering resources unproductive (Chapter 9);
- by continually emitting the random messages produced by perpetual disorder.

3. At a deeper level, the processes of creation brought out in the second part seem to be the twins of the processes of destruction, and to bring the market mechanism back to that of the reference model.

Thus Chapter 9 suggests the following analysis: there exist, at the beginning of each time period, two technologies and two categories of labour (the technicians and the unskilled), but any technician who accepts unskilled work has a certain probability of losing his professional skills and of being definitively reduced to the status of an unskilled labourer.[1] Evolution may then lead to the disappearance of technicians from the market and to the elimination of the corresponding technology. The history of economics furnishes numerous examples of these dynamics of un-learning.

In the same way, as I have already mentioned, Chapter 10 allows us easily to imagine a process by which a union which initially existed on a market may be destroyed. It is enough for the firms, having signed with the union, to imitate the betrayal of one of them and to appear independently one after the other with a certain probability on the free market; they then progressively erode the confidence the employees have in their union to the point that the latter disappears . . .

These few remarks on the destructive capacity of the market, a capacity that has been rather overlooked so far in this volume, naturally lead us to an attempt to specify the content of the concept of self-organization as it might be defined for the science of economics.

Self-Organization

The term as it appears before us is a juxtaposition of two words. Two words which are not entirely clear, neither the first, nor the second.

The prefix 'self' affirms the existence, in the system under consideration, of processes likely to lead, without the intervention of outside agents, to the appearance of an organization. But these processes, when we look closely at them, seem to belong to three different categories:

- the involuntary processes, which lead to an organization which the actors neither anticipated nor wanted (thus the workers and firms in Chapter 2 were at no time conscious of participating in the formation of a single salary leading to a double dichotomy of workers and jobs);
- the voluntary processes which assume that at least one agent formed the project of creating or modifying an organization (this is the case when, for example, an employer in a duopolistic structure tries to take-over his competitor);

---

[1] These days a related phenomenon can be observed in the case of workers who have experienced unemployment of long duration.

- the mixed processes in which there coexist both the germ of an organization in search of an institutional project and the multiple actors likely to contribute their co-operation but without any positive desire to see the project through (the model on the endogenous formation of a union perfectly illustrates this type of process).

It is too early to assert the pertinence of this typology. Nevertheless, the models in this book confirm that the significance of these processes is to be sought in the complexity of the social context, a complexity which forces the agents to dispose of only partial information and to imagine only imperfectly the consequences of their behaviour.

But what is meant by 'organization'? The answer is not simple. Have the preceding chapters not led me to employ the term—perhaps too freely—to designate phenomena as diverse as a simple sorting process, the existence of a union, and the presence of links between beliefs and prices? This observation suggests a very broad definition: there is the appearance of organization every time a relation which did not exist initially is created among the elements of an economic system. In other words, the concept takes on a differential nature and assumes dynamics.

This attempt at semantic analysis is, however, not sufficient for marking off the boundaries of a theory on self-organization in economics. To do so, it is necessary to think about the connection this theory may have to two other approaches that are in a state of development, that of economic evolution and that of institutional economics.

The analogy to biology permits clarification of the first problem. Does the theory of evolution of the species not include multiple branches as different as palaeontology and molecular biology? From this point of view, the theory of self-organization in economics is concerned with elementary micro-economic mechanisms likely to be at the base of an evolution of the whole. It therefore constitutes in a way the 'molecular biology' branch of a—potential—general theory of economic evolution.

As for its relationship to institutional economics, it may be explained with the help of the following statement. Like every discipline, institutional economics includes statics and dynamics. It is with the latter that the theory of self-organization will greatly overlap. The size of this overlap will depend on the exact meaning it will seem desirable to give the concepts of institution and organization. At this time, as I am finishing this book, the distinction is not yet clear in my mind. I would tend to define institution in a more restrictive manner: perhaps as a set of rules meeting certain objectives and applying to a set of agents. From this point of view a union or a company is incontestably an institution, but what about a conceptual model shared by individuals? I must admit that in this respect the vocabulary in the second part of the book lacks rigour at times and is not always consistent with the above statement. We are not sure, moreover, that this subject is of any greater importance than knowing the sex of the angels. Let us build pertinent models, and we shall see what macro-concepts may be brought out.

But let us next turn our attention to various aspects of the building of these models.

Problems of Modelling

Most of the results presented in this book have been obtained through a family of models, the main characteristics of which are the decomposition of time in a succession of periods, the introduction of a finite number of agents, the direct representation of random events concerning each agent, the limitation of values to whole numbers, and the authorization to adapt only by unit steps expectations, demands, or prices.

This type of modelling has simultaneous advantages and drawbacks. The main advantage results from the fact that it reproduces the sequence of steps as lived by every agent while describing precisely the set of relations between agents within the framework of the market. Hence the absence of those shadowy areas which make the meaning of some models of market dynamics pretty unclear.

But this advantage is limited by several drawbacks:

- the model has to be completely specified, which compels us to introduce many assumptions, some of which may seem arbitrary;
- the use of discrete values generates some parasitic phenomena without economic meaning (equilibrium salary defined up to one unit as in Chapter 3, and the occurrence of a ring of individuals always unsatisfied as in Chapter 9, to quote only two examples);

- the proofs of properties cannot rely on some theorems of Markov processes which are only valid for continuous models.

These proofs have until now been based on the construction of paths having a positive probability and leading to stable states, which, according to existing theorems, is sufficient to assure convergence towards such states. These proofs are simple as far as their principles are concerned, but they become heavier and heavier as the models become richer. Using this technique, it does not seem possible to deal with more complex models than those introduced in Chapter 6.

It would undoubtedly be interesting to look for types of models avoiding these drawbacks, but until now our efforts have been unsuccessful.

Dealing with Time

This issue brings up two problems which the book has left in the shadows.

1. What is the historic duration of those unitary periods which enter into the dynamics of the models? A day, a month, a year? On the one hand we know, thanks to work in experimental economics, that convergence to a stable state may be very rapid—a few moves—in laboratory conditions. On the other hand, routine observation has shown us markets with very different reaction times:

- operators on the stock market often decide hour by hour;
- retailers, except in fruits and vegetables, rarely modify their prices with greater frequency than every fortnight;
- suppliers of heavy industrial equipment generally reason in terms of a year while remaining capable of adapting in a few hours on specific contracts.

Hence it is possible to conjecture that not only is the elementary duration highly variable from one market to another, but it may, for the same market, evolve in time under the effect of exogenous and endogenous influences.

But the problem of historical duration implies another question: when is it pertinent to impose the same unitary period on different phenomena which enter into the model? The model on creating skills in Chapter 9 perfectly illustrates this question. It submits, in fact, three groups of processes to the same frequency: the searching, negotiation, and adaptation processes of the labour-market, the processes of going from unskilled labourer to technician, and the processes by which a firm changes its technology. It is clear that these three groups do not have the same time constants. The theory of economic self-organization will in the future have to apply itself, on this point, to accounting for reality, with greater accuracy.

The second problem in dealing with time stems directly from this proposition.

2. How does one choose sub-systems in equilibrium and disequilibrium and articulate them in a model? The case of the endogenous formation of a union can be taken as an example on this subject: in this model it was accepted that, at the end of each period, the free market was in equilibrium and the corresponding salary s_t became common knowledge. In other words, the economic system was separated into two coupled sub-systems:

- a sub-system with rapid dynamics, the free market, which receives from the other sub-system a supply curve and a demand curve and sends it an equilibrium wage in response;
- a sub-system with slow dynamics which uses the equilibrium wage as an element of change in the agents' behaviour and sends some of these agents back on to the free market.

The methods of complex systems decomposition have long been known to physicists and practised by them. They respond to two distinct motivations which are more or less compatible:

- the necessity of building models as simple as possible (the assumption that certain sub-systems attain their equilibrium instantaneously pays off quite well in this respect since it simplifies the exits of the sub-systems and reduces that part of the model which is, strictly speaking, dynamic);
- the desire to take into account the different reaction times which characterize the various linkages in economics.

The development of research on economic dynamics will naturally result in a flowering of models, with the coexistence of coupled sub-systems having distinct dynamics.

The Introduction of Limited Rationality Behaviour

The models in this book generally use two means for representing reality which must not be confused:

- recourse to decentralized procedures excluding either the existence of an auctioneer, or the agents' possession of all necessary information in the form of common knowledge;
- the agents' adoption of limited rationality behaviour patterns.

In fact, as soon as decentralized procedures are used, self-organization phenomena may appear, even if the agents are capable of strategic behaviour making full use of the information individually available.

Naturally, introducing less rational behaviour enlarges the scope of stable states and may even destroy the existence of such states.

Hence the interest in continuing research in two directions:

- on the one hand, as proposed by Lainé,[2] by exploring models with decentralizable or self-organizable procedures in which the actors adopt strategic behaviour;
- on the other hand, as suggested in Chapter 5, by attempting to build a classification of limited rationality behaviour and by analysing the influence of the chosen types on the dynamics of models with decentralizable or self-organizable procedures.

Naturally, when the agents behave with limited rationality, a distinction must be made between models with homogeneous agents—that is, those whose behaviour is of the same type—and those with heterogeneous agents. As several chapters of the book have in fact shown, a small number of agents acting in a certain way may be sufficient to destroy states which would be stable in their absence. We see outlined here the role of important figures in micro-economics. It seems to me that we are unfortunately still far from a coherent classification of limited rationality behaviour, even if the notion of a finite automat did prove productive in game theory. I have therefore adopted, in this book, a very pragmatic approach by choosing, with discretion, the rules of behaviour which seemed reasonable to me as seen from the agents' point of view. This approach may be useful for clearing some ground; it in no way

---

[2] A speech at the author's seminar on decentralizable and self-organizable procedures.

diminishes the interest of a rigorous analysis of the concept of limited rationality.

Introducing simultaneously into a model behaviour of limited rationality and decentralizable or self-organizable procedures, currently results in multiplying the hypotheses necessary for a precise definition of the model and gives the formalization an aspect both complex and arbitrary which leaves us unsatisfied.

Under these circumstances, two paths of research are worth exploring:

- the first consists of a broad use of simulation methods in order to estimate quickly the probable qualitative influences of varied rules of limited rationality behaviour, to detect the essential parameters within these rules, and to make a better choice of the models worthy of careful mathematical treatment;
- the second proposes the building of more general models based on less particular rules as to behaviour and negotiation processes in the hope of ending up with theorems of broader significance.

There is only one certainty: the staggering development that the cognitive sciences are presently experiencing will perhaps suggest to economists, on condition that they accept the weighty task of reinterpretation, pertinent behavioural hypotheses.

The Role of Chance

Chance is omnipresent in all the models in this book, in various forms and with diverse consequences.

It may be exogenous as in the case of the quality of wine or the emergence of sunspots. It may be linked to the transmission of information during the agents' encounters. It may stem from the conditions under which a new technical innovation was discovered. It may show up on the occasion of an actor's change in skills. It may be incorporated into the decision-makers' rules of behaviour when the former explore models of belief or modifications of their demands. There is, moreover, no reason to consider the list of cases encountered in this book to be exhaustive. This observation inspires a warning: nothing would be more incorrect than to assimilate models of self-organization to a simple extension of 'search' models. Certainly, the latter are the first to have begun dynamic analysis of individual behaviour on the market, but their partial nature did not help us to understand the variety and significance of chance phenomena in global dynamics.

Upon finishing this book, it seems to me easier to grasp the meaning, for the science of economics, of the notion of an event in the way that Prigogine and Stengers conceived it. In the initial model in Chapter 2, there are chance happenings but no pertinent events. In fact, chance happenings make the market progress to a stable state with a single price, but in no way influence the course of history. It is completely different in models in other chapters (Chapters 3 and 9, for example) in which two types of chance occurrences appear:

- those which have no certain consequences and are limited, at the most, to modifying the probabilities of future histories without altering the range of histories;
- those which generate irreversible consequences and definitely lock a system into a restricted range of possibilities, thus constituting actual events.

An event therefore assumes the conjunction of two elements: a chance occurrence, which may be microscopic, and the presence of a context which generates cumulative consequences giving the occurrence a macroscopic follow-up. Two analogies immediately come to mind:

- The first is from physics, and, in this respect, is only mentioned here to jog the memory; it is based on the observation that every explosion implies two stages: the lighting of the fuse which starts off a reaction in the powder, and the spreading of that chain reaction at such speed that it gives off considerable power.
- The second is of a social nature; it concerns strikes, revolutions, military disasters, and historic disturbances. At the beginning there is often a chance occurrence, apparently modest: the firing of a worker or an accident on the job, a concession made too late by those in power, a number of deaths caused by the forces of order under unclear circumstances, the breakthrough of a few enterprising military officers like Rommel at Caporetto, the appearance of an unexpected figure like Gorbachev, etc., but this chance event only produces immense effects because the conditions for a cumulative tilting of the scale have been united—a seed of discontent among workers, a government's loss of legitimacy in the eyes of its citizens,

a lassitude within the troops, or a failure in their command, a centralized power structure allowing reforms to be started at the top, etc.

The Influence of Exceptional Figures

In current micro-economic theory, managers are interchangeable. Maximizing a net income, a mathematical profit expectation, or, at the limit, a utility function, the only influence they have over the succession of events is that resulting from the resources that some or others control. But, in Chapters 5 and 11, we had a glimpse of a wholly different approach starting with the two following premises (Lesourne 1989):

1. Every agent carrying out an economic role has a personality expressed through:

- his own objectives which do not necessrily identify with those of his superiors;
- a more or less subtle capacity for judging the objectives, the resources, and the beliefs of other actors;
- an aptitude, more or less well developed, for obtaining the support (in objectives and efficiency) of those he commands;
- an imagination more or less sensitive to discovering innovative conduct;
- an ability to calculate, permitting the designing of more or less complicated rules for decision-making.

2. The conditions needed for an agent to accede to an economic role are governed by procedures whose execution is influenced by chance phenomena; whether it be designating a jury or establishing a list of candidates, holding debates or conducting a vote.

Thus, in 1866, on the threshold of the war against Prussia and Piedmont, the Austrian monarchy had the choice between two generals, Benedek and the Archduke Albert, to command its armies in Bohemia and Milan. After much hesitation, it was decided to send the first to the German front and the second to the Italian front. It is difficult to admit that such a choice[3] did not result from factors which were for a large part imponderable. It was undoubtedly

---

[3] Which I in no way claim to be an explanation for the defeat of Sadowa or the victory of Custozza.

the same at the time John XXIII was elected. And how can one
believe that the Soviet Politburo had perfect information on Gorbachev as a public figure when he was designated as Secretary-
General?

At the more modest level of designating company presidents, the
same processes are at work. No one has demonstrated it better than
Parkinson in the entertaining short novel in which he recounts the
misadventure of a technostructure which made every effort to
ensure the accession to the presidential chair of the executive who
was the most conformist, the most unimaginative, and the most
faithful to traditional objectives, only to discover—too late—a
strong, creative personality which had been hidden for decades!

By relating these premises to what was said on the role of chance
in the preceding paragraphs, it is possible to formulate with precision
the question of the eventual influence of an important figure in the
evolution of an economy. In fact, depending on the circumstances,
three situations are conceivable, within the framework of the same
model, as to the consequences of the emergence of an important
figure, whoever it may be, in a decision-making position. This
emergence may:

- be without influence on the course of events to come since the
  outcome of the future random path is determined;
- modify, slightly or not, but in a reversible manner, the probability
  of the diverse trajectories, other figures—or other chance
  occurrences—being likely one day to undo what has been
  done;
- introduce an actual rupture in the evolution of the economy by
  definitively eliminating a more or less important fraction of the
  possible future.

That it is useful for the science of economics to delve deeper into
this question goes without saying; but it is for the research of
tomorrow to explore this area, which is as vast as it is difficult.

From Market Dynamics to Hierarchy Dynamics

The reader has undoubtedly been convinced for some time that this
book constitutes but one quite modest step in the study of the
creation of economic organizations. To go beyond that, it is not

enough to gain deeper understanding of market dynamics, it is also necessary to deal with the analysis of the dynamics of hierarchies, notably those of the firm. By most often reducing the latter to a single centre of decision-making and a production function, economists perceive it essentially as an actor subjected to threats from without (rivals' strategies, changes in demand, the decisions of the State, etc.), trying to ward off these threats in order to ensure its survival.

But sociologists and management specialists have long known that the relations betwen the firm and the outside world make up but one side of reality. The other side concerns the interactions which take place within the firm among staff members or between them and the goods and services they provide.

From there on, if we adopt an evolutionist point of view, we are forced to observe:

- that on both sides of the 'membrane' which contains the firm, the processes of destruction and creation of order are at work;
- that these processes are not independent, and that there is constant interference between internal and external processes.

Over the last few years economic theories on the firm (Holmstrom and Tirole 1989) have multiplied, offering from here on an interesting basis of departure for the development of the economics of order and disorder. Under these circumstances, attempts at model-building are imaginable in at least three directions:

1. The first path might, at an initial stage, deal with the operating of a firm, limited to a team[4] of two directors. At a dynamics level, the object would be to examine how the directors by meeting every T periods could progressively improve, through trial and error, their rules of individual behaviour and co-operation, each set of rules being determined for T periods at least. Naturally, as the research progressed, it would be possible to introduce conflicts between the directors, conflicts stemming from their differences of opinion. In the second stage, the analysis would be concentrated on the evolution of a duopoly in which each firm would be composed of three people (for example, a director and two assistant directors). The rules of individual behaviour and co-ordination being modified in view of experience, for each of the firms in the duopoly, the dynamics of competition between the two would be studied.

---

[4] In the sense given the term by Marschak and Radner (1972).

2. A second path would consist of building global models of firms linking internal and external processes of creation and destruction (Lesourne 1989). It would be desirable to examine first of all, from a limited rationality point of view, a model already greatly studied in other disciplines: it describes an organization which in order to survive must dispose of reserves $R(t) > 0$. This organization may be active or passive. When it is passive, it consumes, for internal operations, volume a of reserves per unit of time and no addition to the reserves is made. When it is active, it consumes in addition volume b of its reserves per unit of time, but has a probability $p(0 < p < 1)$ of increasing its reserves by c units. The problem is to explore the consequences, for the survival of the organization, of the state of its information and the nature of the rules of empirical behaviour it adopts or, with some trial and error, progressively elaborates.

It would also be desirable to study models with several random elements in which the firm, for example, controls imperfectly both demand, in spite of adaptation of its sales price, and staff, in spite of adaptation of the wages paid. Another category of models could be built to explore, through application to the firm, that property well known in systemics, according to which there are two ways for an organization to die out: by multiplying innovations at such a rate that it does not learn to evaluate environmental reactions, and by refusing to modify its behaviour with such constancy that it becomes less and less adapted to reality.

3. There remains, naturally, the royal road, opened up by Williamson (1975, 1989), that of the study of social arbitration between market and hierarchy. But the idea is not to follow this path with the mere intention of enumerating the respective merits of these two forms of organization. The object must be to understand how, under the pressure of agents, market and hierarchy generate each other, a hierarchy organizing itself out of a market, eventually destroying the latter in order to participate in the birth of a vaster market, before perhaps dissolving in its turn into more elementary components and being reabsorbed by the market.

Ah! But it will be exciting to be a theoretical economist at the dawn of the next century!

References

AKERLOF, G. (1970), 'The market for lemons: qualitative uncertainty and the market mechanism', *Quarterly Journal of Economics*, 84.

ALCHIAN, A. A. (1950), 'Uncertainty, evolution and economic theory', *Journal of Political Economy*, 58.

ALLAIS, M. (1981), 'La théorie générale des surplus', *Économies et sociétés*, Jan.–May.

ALLEN, P. (1980*a*), 'The evolutionary paradigm of dissipative structures', in E. Jantsch, AAAA selected Symposium, Westview Press.

—— (1980*b*), 'Self-organization in human systems', *Revue belge de statistique, d'informatique et de recherche opérationnelle*.

—— (1981), 'Urban evolution viewed as a self-organizing non-linear system', *Communication to the yearly meeting of the British Regional Science Association*.

ARROW, K. (1962), 'The economic implications of learning by doing', *Review of Economic Studies*, 29.

—— and DEBREU, G. (1954), 'Existence of equilibrium for a competitive economy', *Econometrica*, 22.

ARTHUR, B. (1989), 'Competing technologies, increasing returns and lock-in by historical events', *Economic Journal*.

ASHBY, W. R. (1952), *Design for a Brain: The Origin of Adaptive Behaviour* (London: Chapman and Hall).

—— (1956), *An Introduction to Cybernetics* (London: Chapman and Hall).

ATLAN, H. (1972), *L'Organisation biologique et la théorie de l'information* (Paris: Herman).

AZARIADIS, C. (1981), 'Self-fulfilling Prophecies', *Journal of Economic Theory*, 25.

—— and GUESNERIE, R. (1982), 'Prophécies créatrices et persistance des théories', *Revue economique*, 5.

AXELL, B. (1977), 'Search market equilibrium', *Scandinavian Journal of Economics*, 79.

BALDWIN, W. L., and SCOTT, J. T. (1987), 'Market structure and technological change', *Fundamentals of Pure and Applied Economics* (Harwood Academic Publishers).

BATESON, G. (1951), *Communication: The Social Matrix of Psychiatry* (New York: Norton).

BEER, S. (1959), *Cybernetics and Management* (London: English Universities Press).

—— (1966), *Decision and Control: The Meaning of Operational Research and Management Cybernetics* (London: Wiley).

BIRNBAUM, P. and LECAS, J. (1986), *Sur l'individualisme* (Paris: Presses de la Fondation Nationale des Sciences Politiques).

BOUDON, R. (1977), *Effets pervers et ordre social* (Paris: Presses Universitaires de France).

BOULDING, K. (1981), *Evolutionary Economics* (London: Sage).

BRAUDEL, F. (1979), *Civilisation matérielle: économie et capitalisme $xv^{ème}-xviii^{ème}$ siècles, Le Temps du monde* (Paris: Armand Colin).

BRILLOUIN, L. (1949), 'Life, thermodynamics and cybernetics', *American Scientist*, reproduced in W. Buckley, *Modern Systems Research for the Behavioral Scientist* (Chicago: Aldine Publishing Company, 1969).

BUTTERS, G. (1977), 'Equilibrium distributions for sales and advertising prices', *Review of Economic Studies*.

CARON-SALMONA, H. (1985), 'Equilibre sur le marché d'un bien en information imparfaite: une analyse de la littérature, *Économie appliquée*.

—— and LESOURNE, J (1987), 'Dynamics of a retail market with search processes', *European Economic Review*, 31.

CHIAPPORI, P. A. (1984), 'Sélection naturelle et rationalité absolue des entreprises', *Revue économique*.

—— and GUESNERIE, R. (1987), *Self-fulfilling Theories and Sunspot Equilibria: The One Dimensional Case* (Paris: Éditions de la maison des sciences de l'homme).

COASE, R. H. (1937), 'The nature of the firm', *Economica*, 4.

COMMONS, J. R. (1934), *Institutional Economics* (Madison, Wis.: University of Wisconsin Press).

COMPTE, O., LESOURNE, J. and LEVY, B. (1989), 'La formation endogène d'un syndicat sur le marché du travail', *Economie appliquée*.

CONLISK, J. (1989), 'Optimisation, adaptation and random innovations in a model of economic growth', paper presented at the International symposium on evolutionary dynamics and non-linear economics, Apr. Austin, Texas.

CYERT, R. M., and MARCH, J. G. (1963), *A Behavioral Theory of the Firm* (Englewood Cliffs, NJ: Prentice Hall).

DAVID, P. (1988), *The Future of Path-Dependent Equilibrium Economics* (Center for Economic Policy Research, Stanford University).

DAY, R. H. (1986), 'On endogenous preferences and adaptive economizing', in R. H. Day and G. Eliason (eds.), *The Dynamics of Market Economies* (Amsterdam: North Holland).

—— and ELIASSON, G. (1986), *The Dynamics of Market Economics* (Amsterdam: North Holland).

DEBREU, G. (1959), *Theory of Value* (New York: Wiley).

DENNIEL, P. Y. (1989), 'Le concept d'organisation: du système aux modèles', Ph.D. thesis Université de Droit, d'Économie et des Sciences d'Aix-Marseille.

DEUTSCH, K. W. (1963), *The Nerves of Government* (New York: Free Press of Glencoe).

DIAMON, P. A. (1971), 'A model of price adjustment', *Journal of Economic Theory*, June.

DUPUY, J. P. (1982), *Ordres et désordres* (Paris: Le Seuil).

—— (1988), 'Common knowledge et sens commun', *Cahiers du CREA*, 11.

EASTON, D. (1965), *A Systems Analysis of Political Life* (New York: Wiley).

ELIASSON, G. (1977), 'Competition and market processes in a simulation model of the Swedish economy', *American Economic Review*, 67.

FARBER, H. S. (1986), 'The analysis of union behaviour', in O. Ashenfelter and R. Layard (eds.), *Handbook of Labor Economics* (Amsterdam: North Holland).

FISHER, D. S., GRINSTEIN, M., and KHURANA, A. (1988), *Theory of Random Magnets*, Physics Today.

FISHER, F. M. (1970), 'Quasi competitive price adjustment by individual firms: a preliminary paper', *Quarterly Journal of Economics*, Apr.

—— (1973), 'Stability and competitive equilibrium in two models of search and individual price adjustment', *Journal of Economic Theory*, 6.

FREEMAN, C. (1974), *The Economics of Industrial Innovation* (Harmondsworth: Penguin).

FUDENBERG, D., and TIROLE, J. (1986), 'Dynamic models of oligopoly', in *Fundamentals of Pure and Applied Economics* (London: Harwood Academic Publishers).

FUTIA, C. (1980), 'Schumpeterian competition', *Quarterly Journal of Economics*, 94.

GREEN, H. S., and HURST, C. A. (1964), *Order-Disorder Phenomena* (New York: Wiley).

GREEN, J., (1972), 'Information, efficiency and equilibrium', Discussion paper 284, Harvard Institute of Economic Research.

—— (1977), 'The non-existence of informational equilibria', *Review of Economic Studies*, 44.

GROSSMAN, S. J., 'An introduction to the theory of rational expectations under asymmetric information', *Review of Economic Studies*, 54.

HART, D. O., and KREPS, D. M. (1986), 'Price destabilizing speculation', *Journal of Political Economy*, 94.

HART, O. (1988), 'The nature and extent of the firm', Fisher-Schulz lecture, European Meeting of the Econometric Society.

References

HEY, J. D. (1974), 'Price adjustment in an atomistic market', *Journal of Economic Theory*, 8.

—— and MCKENNA, C. (1981), 'Consumer search with uncertain product quality', *Journal of Political Economy*.

HOLSTROM, B. K., and TIROLE, J. (1989), 'The theory of the firm', in *Handbook of Industrial Organization*, i, ed. R. Schmalensee and R. D. Willig (Amsterdam: North Holland).

HURWICZ, L., RADNER, R., and REITER, S. (1975), 'A stochastic decentralized resource allocation process, part I', *Econometrica*, 43.

JACQUEMIN, A. (1986), *Sélection et pouvoir dans la nouvelle économie industrielle* (Paris: Economica-Cabay).

JORDAN, J., and RADNER, R. (1982), 'Rational expectations in microeconomic models: an overview', *Journal of Economic Theory*, 26.

KIRMAN, A. (1988), *On Ants and Markets* (Florence: European University Instititue).

KNIGHT, F. (1921), *Risk, Uncertainty and Profit* (Boston, Mass.: Houghton Mifflin).

LAFFOND, G. (1989), 'La révélation de la qualité par les prix sur un marché en auto-organisation', *Économie appliquée*.

—— and LESOURNE, J. (1981), 'Market dynamics and search processes with information costs', *Communication to the European Meeting of the Econometric Society*, Amsterdam.

—— and —— (1985a), 'Un exemple d'auto-organisation: la création de capacités professionnelles par le marché du travail', *Économie appliquée*.

—— and —— (1985b), 'Market dynamics and search processes with information costs', *Économie appliquée*.

—— and —— (1988), 'La dynamique d'un marché avec transmission d'information par les prix', *Essais en l'honneur d'Edmond Malinvaud* (Paris: Economica).

—— and —— (1989), *A Dynamic Model with Sunspot Stable States* (Paris: CNAM).

LAFFONT, J. J. (1985), 'Cours de théorie micro-économique, vol. II', *Économie de l'incertain et de l'information* (Paris: Economica).

LAINÉ, J. (1987), 'Échange et communication: essai sur l'efficacité parétienne dans une économie contrainte', Ph.D. thesis, Rennes University.

—— (1989), 'Processus d'échanges bilatéraux et auto-organisation du marché', *Économie appliquée*.

LASLIER, J. F. (1989a), 'Développement des entreprises et évolution de la concurrence', *Économie appliquée*.

—— (1989b), 'Diffusion d'informations et évaluations séquentielles', *Économie appliquée*.

—— and LESOURNE, J. (1989), 'Rendements croissants et dynamique d'un marché', *Économie appliquée*.

LESOURNE, J. (1976), *Les systèmes du destin* (Paris: Dalloz).

—— (1985), 'Le marché et l'auto-organisation', *Économie appliquée*.

—— (1986), 'L'auto-organisation et le marché', in M. Boiteux, T. de Montbrial, and B. Munier, *Marchés, capital et incertitudes: essais en l'honneur de Maurice Allais* (Paris: Economica).

—— (1989*a*), 'À propos d'un apologue militaire: le rôle des personnalités dans un processus historique', *Économie appliquée*.

—— (1989*b*), 'L'entreprise en lutte sur deux fronts', *Économie appliquée*.

—— (1989*c*), 'L'état des recherches sur l'ordre et le désordre en micro-économie', *Économie appliquée*.

—— and LAFFOND, G. (1979), 'Market dynamics and search processes', *Communication to the European Meeting of the Econometric Society*, Athens.

—— and RENAULT, E. (1985), 'Auto-organisation et dispersion géographique des marchés', *Économie appliquée* (a first version was presented to the European Meeting of the Econometric Society, Amsterdam, 1981).

LUCAS, R. E. (1972), 'Expectations and the neutrality of money', *Journal of Economic Theory*, 4.

McMINN, R. D. (1980), 'Search and market equilibrium', *Journal of Political Economy*.

MARSCHAK, J. and RADNER, R. (1972), *Economic Theory of Teams* (New Haven, Conn.: Yale University Press).

MATURANA, H. R. (1970), 'The neurophysiology of cognition', in P. Garvin, *Cognition: A Multiple View* (New York: Spartan Books).

MESAROVIC, M. D. and ECKMAN, D. P. (1961), 'On some basic concepts of the general systems theory', *Proceedings of the Third International Conference on Cybernetics*, Namur.

—— and TAKAHARA, Y. (1975), *General Systems Theory: Mathematical Foundations* (New York: Academic Press).

MILGROM, P. and STOKEY, N. (1982), 'Information, trade and common knowledge', *Journal of Economic Theory*, 26.

MORIN, E. (1977, 1980), *La Méthode*, i. *La Nature de la nature* (Paris: Le Seuil); ii. *La Vie de la vie* (Paris: Le Seuil).

NELSON, R. N., and WINTERS, S. G. (1982), *An Evolutionary Theory of Economic Change* (Cambridge, Mass.: Belknap Press of Harvard University Press).

NICOLIS, Q., and PRIGOGINE, I. (1977), *Self-Organization in Non Equilibrium Systems, from Dissipative Structures to Order through Fluctuations* (New York: Wiley).

ORLÉAN, A. (1989*a*), 'Comportements mimétiques et diversité des opinions sur les marchés financiers', in P. Artus and H. Bourguinat, *Théorie économique et crises des marchés financiers* (Paris: Economica).

—— 'Mimetic contagion and speculative bubbles', *Theory and Decision*, 27.

References

PARKINSON, C. N. (1957), *Parkinson's Law or the Pursuit of Progress* (London: John Murray).

PERROUX, F. (1975), *Unités actives et mathématiques nouvelles, révision de la théorie de l'équilibre économique général* (Paris: Dunod).

PRIGOGINE, I. (1962), *Introduction à la thermodynamique des processus irréversibles* (French trans., Paris: Dunod, 1969).

—— and STENGERS, I. (1988), *Entre le temps et l'éternité* (Paris: Fayard).

RADNER, R. (1979), 'Rational expectations equilibrium: generic existence and the information revealed by prices', *Econometrica*, 47.

REINGANUM, J. (1979), 'A simple model of equilibrium price dispersion', *Journal of Political Economy*.

RILEY, J. (1979), 'Informational equilibrium', *Econometrica*.

ROSENBERG, N. (1976), *Perspectives on Technology* (Cambridge: Cambridge University Press).

ROTHSCHILD, M. and STIGLITZ, J. (1976), 'Equilibrium in competitive insurance markets: an essay on the economics of imperfect information', *Quarterly Journal of Economics*.

SALMONA, H. (1985), 'Équilibre sur le marché d'un bien en information imparfaite: une analyse de la littérature', *Économie appliquée*.

SALOP, S., and STIGLITZ, J. (1977), 'Bargains and ripoffs: a model of monopolistically competitive price dispersion', *Review of Economic Studies*, 94.

—— and —— (1982), 'The theory of sales: a simple model of equilibrium price dispersion with identical agents', *American Economic Review*, Dec.

SCHELLING, T. (1978), *Micromotives and Macrobehaviour* (New York: Norton).

SCHUMPETER, J. A. (1934; 1st edn. 1912), *The Theory of Economic Development* (Cambridge, Mass.: Harvard University Press).

—— (1950; 1st edn. 1942), *Capitalism, Socialism and Democracy* (New York: Harper).

SIMON, H. A. (1957), *Models of Man* (New York: Wiley).

SMALLWOOD, D., and CONLISK, J. (1979), 'Product quality in markets where consumers are imperfectly informed', *Quarterly Journal of Econometrics*.

SOMPOLINSKY, H. (1988), *Statistical Mechanics of Neural Networks*, Physics Today.

SPENCE, M. (1974), *Market Signalling: Information Transfer in Hiring and Related Screening Processes* (Cambridge, Mass.: Harvard University Press).

STIGLER, G. (1961), 'The economics of information', *Journal of Political Economy*, 69.

STIGLITZ, J. (1979), 'Equilibrium in product market with imperfect information', *American Economic Review*, May.

VARELA, F. J. (1979), *Principles of Biological Autonomy* (New York: Elsevier).

VON BERTALANFFY, L. (1968), *General System Theory: Foundation, Development, Applications* (New York: G. Braziller).

VON FOERSTER, H. (1960), 'On self-organizing systems and their environments', in M. C. Yovits and S. Cameron, *Self-Organizing Systems* (New York: Pergamon Press).

VON HAYEK, F. (1945), 'The use of knowledge in society', *American Economic Review*, 35.

WALLISER, B. (1985), *Anticipations, équilibres et rationalité économique* (Paris: Calmann-Levy).

WALRAS, L. (1874), *Éléments d'économie politique pure* (Lausanne: Corbaz).

WILDE, L. L., and SCHWARTZ, A. (1979), 'Equilibrium comparison stopping', *Review of Economic Studies*, 46.

WILLIAMSON, O. E. (1975), *Markets and Hierarchies: Analysis and Antitrust Applications* (New York: Free Press).

—— (1989), 'Transaction cost economics', in *Handbook of Industrial Organisation*, i. ed. R. Schamalensee and R. D. Willig (Amsterdam: North Holland).

WITT, U. (1986a), 'Coordination of individual economic activities', *Économie appliquée*.

—— (1986b), *Individualistische Grundlagen der evolutorischen Ökonomik* (Tübingen: Mohr).

ZELENY, M. (1980), *Autopoiesis, Dissipative Structures and Spontaneous Social Orders* (Boulder, Colo.: Westview).

—— (1981), *Autopoiesis: A Theory of Living Organization* (New York: North Holland).

INDEX

Index

Hey, J. D. 27 n., 91
hierarchies 6, 7, 12, 14, 15, 183
   dynamics 194–6
hiring 27, 36, 144
history 129, 131, 140, 156, 158, 163
   future 2, 192; probabilities 192
   individual 21
   leading to multiple equilibria 58
   random 101
   stable state and 107
   sunspots 138
   uncertainties 68
   value dependent upon 124
Holmstrom, B. K. 195
human will 2, 38
Hurst, C. A. 127 n.
Hurwicz, L. 7
hypotheses 105, 156, 172, 174
   behavioural 6, 191
   beliefs 138–9
   circulation of information 72
   enumeration of 25–33
   general theory of systems 4
   institutional economics 6–7
   jumps of scale 70–1, 75–6
   limited rationality 21
   negotiation and demand
     adjustment 65
   observations 66, 139
   rational expectations 20
   recruitment agency 118
   salary 74
   simple market 34, 37–8, 39, 52
   stable state 77–8, 86
   technical 151
   traditional market 83, 91, 92–3, 94
   see also models

imitation 124, 130, 165, 177, 178, 180
income 35, 59, 60, 115, 119, 154
   see also earnings; salaries; wages
individual behaviour 19–25, 50, 53, 54,
   153–4
   consequences 38
   describing 65
   dynamic analysis 192
   information and 30
   job applicants 66
   resilience of the market and 47
   rules 195
   theories 32
   young and old 133
individuals:

active 66, 67; with potential
   mobility 68
   anticipative 124
   capable 143
   contacts between 73
   employable 145
   imitative 124
   inside 75, 76
   passive 66–7
   promotable 143, 144, 145–6
   promoted 143, 144
   see also buyers; craftsmen;
     entrepreneurs; individual
     behaviour; sellers; workers
influences:
   direct and indirect 123
   exceptional figures 193–4
   exogenous and endogenous 188
information 74–5, 83, 94, 124
   access 31, 179
   acquisition 51
   agents and 131, 190; ability to obtain
     114; ability to process 10;
     gathering or diffusing 28
   anonymous 121
   circulation 70, 72, 76–7, 80
   complete 101–4
   discovery rendered impossible or
     costly 9
   exchanges 12, 13
   extensive 30, 39, 47, 52
   faith in 129
   false 122
   imperfect 7, 165
   incomplete 101, 104–7, 165
   inexact 119, 121
   new 122
   partial 186
   perfect 26, 51, 194
   present 152
   public 98, 119
   revealing 122
   search process 36, 38, 45, 46–7, 92,
     116
   spreading 179
information costs 64–5, 81, 116, 121,
   123
   absence 38
   model with 62–9, 113, 115
   payment 32
   positive 91
   search 64, 66, 83
   substantial 55

210
Index

organization(s) (*cont.*):
  closed 43, 44, 46
  diversity 162
  partial 109
  see also self-organization
Orléan, A. 124, 130, 131

Parkinson, C. N. 194
Perroux, F. 5, 118
planned economies 16
political parties 160
positions, *see* jobs
preferences 10, 21, 22, 51, 52, 53
  adapting 9
  having 'good' properties 50
  past consumption and 150
prices 10, 21, 23, 50–1, 32, 164
  announcement 125
  beliefs and 186
  bottom 99, 100, 116, 150
  ceiling 83, 101, 116, 118, 150
  conditions 171
  consumer 139–40
  current 120
  dispersion 40 n., 93, 94, 95, 109;
    equilibrium with 29 n., 92;
    stability with 56
  equilibrium 67, 68, 102, 119, 180;
    convergence towards 52, 54;
    monopolistic 91; 'revealing' 97;
    single 94, 134
  flexible 8
  formation 123
  future 120, 133
  guaranteed 160
  high and low 159
  maximum 102, 105, 167
  minimum 88, 102, 105, 108
  monopolistic 91, 93, 96, 110; stable
    state at 92, 94, 95
  quality through 97–108, 109
  retailers and 82–94, 188
  role, in revealing information 122
  sales 82, 176, 196
  setting 34, 136
  single 13, 60, 88, 94, 192
  sunspots and 137, 138
  variability 113
  variations 121
Prigogine, I. 4, 8, 38, 62, 192
privatization 125
probabilities 52, 78, 101, 168–9, 170–1,
  188

discovering jobs 115, 116, 117
diverse trajectories 194
firms and workers 75, 174, 175
forming of opinions 126, 127, 130,
  131, 137
future histories 192
selling 120
skills 142, 143, 184
success in R. & D. 177, 179
uniform, individuals and 36
unions: behaviour 155; and
  firms 154, 185; membership 153
see also stable state
production 80, 147 n., 150, 173, 178
  apparatus 166
  capacity 170, 172, 176, 177
  costs 29 n., 83, 93, 94, 164; unit 82
  factors 8
  first level of 71, 74
  functions 2, 3, 195
  processes 43
productivity 173, 174, 175, 177, 179
  capital 176, 178
  investment 164, 165
  labour 172
profit 22, 38, 74, 84–5, 92, 166–7
  anticipations of 164
  devolution of 165
  distribution 171
  per unit of capacity 176, 178
  reaction to drop in 86
  recruitment agencies 116, 118
  substantial 122
profitability 118, 122, 164
promotion 149

quality 14, 34, 97–108, 150, 164
quantity 14, 84, 119, 134, 164, 180
  choice of 85–6, 136

Radner, R. 7, 97, 195 n.
rationality 8
  bounded 164
  see also limited rationality
recruitment 74, 76, 142, 172, 173, 174
  agencies 113–18, 121, 179
  see also hiring
regularities 51, 52, 159
Reinganum, J. 29, 31 n.
Reiter, S. 7
rents 96, 110, 162
research 181–2, 183

Varela, F. J. 4
von Bertalanffy, L. 4
von Foerster, H. 4
von Hayek, F. 5
voting intentions 125

wages 35, 36–7, 38, 39, 77, 158
  actual 80
  adaptation 196
  demands 44, 48, 121, 142, 151, 152
  dispersion 59, 67, 116, 117
  equilibrium 40, 146, 151, 160, 189;
    maximum 153 n.; minimum 145
  levels 176
  maximum 35, 37, 40, 67, 151 n.
  minimum 35, 40, 44, 149, 151 n., 160
  offer 64, 172
  planned 79
  possible 80
  reservation 72
Walliser, B. 19
Walras, L. 3, 5, 38, 184
Western Europe 80

Wilde, L. L. 92
Williamson, O. E. 6–7, 11, 196
Winters, S. G. 5, 6, 176, 180
Witt, U. 5
work period 36, 48
workers 172, 176
  firms and 39, 42, 63–4, 70–80, 148;
    bottom and ceiling price 116;
    demands 44; independent
    transactions between 36;
    indifference 35; monopolistic
    situation 175; random contact
    between 173
  recruitment agencies and 117, 118,
    121
  unions and 152, 160
  see also craftsmen; technicians

yields 13, 71–81

Zeleny, M. 43, 44

Index compiled by Frank Pert